Soup du Jour

("Soup of the Day")

Healthy Homemade Soups
for All Seasons

By Wendy Esko
Foreword by Gale Jack

One Peaceful World Press
Becket, Massachusetts

Soup du Jour
© 1996 by Wendy Esko

For further information on mail-order sales, wholesale or retail dis-
counts, distribution, translations, and foreign rights, please contact
the publisher:

One Peaceful World Press
P.O. Box 10
Leland Road
Becket, MA 01223
U.S.A.

Telephone (413) 623-2322
Fax (413) 623-8827

First Edition: May 1996
10 9 8 7 6 5 4 3 2 1

ISBN 1–882984–19-6
Printed in U.S.A.

Contents

Foreword

We are in the midst of a worldwide diet and health revolution. As the new millennium approaches, individuals and families around the world are discovering that a diet based on whole cereal grains, fresh vegetables, and other predominantly plant-quality foods is the key not only to maintaining personal health, but also to preserving the natural beauty and health of the planet.

For twenty-five years, Wendy Esko has been in the forefront of this planetary transformation, as a cook, teacher, author, and mother. Thousands of people—including many leading chefs, holistic health care practitioners, and environmentalists—have studied with Wendy. Thousands of others know her through her many cookbooks and increasingly through articles and recipes on the Internet.

In *Soup du Jour*, Wendy turns her attention to the subject of soups, stews, broths, and chowders. As educator Michio Kushi has taught, soup replicates the ancient sea out of which life began. By taking one or two cups or bowls of soup a day, especially soup that has been seasoned with miso or other foods containing enzymes or bacteria, we recreate the early evolutionary development of our species and secure the biological foundation for health, happiness, and peace.

Wendy Esko's soups are healthful, delicious, and endlessly varied. In *Soup du Jour*, the companion to her best-selling cookbook, *Rice Is Nice*, Wendy shares over 100 hearty soups and broths using only whole natural foods and seasonings. As part of a balanced diet and lifestyle, the recipes in this book will go a long way to help you preserve your own health and vitality, as well as that of your family and the earth as a whole.

This cookbook will find a prominent place in my kitchen, as I trust it will in yours. I look forward eagerly to Wendy's next book in her series for One Peaceful World Press.

Gale Jack
Becket, Massachusetts
February 1996

Gale Jack is a cooking teacher at the Kushi Institute, director of the Women's Macrobiotic Society, and author of the best-selling cookbook Amber Waves of Grain *(Japan Publications).*

Introduction

I love preparing soups. Soups are an integral part of a health-ful diet. An endless variety of soups can be made using all-natural ingredients. Soups can be thick and creamy, chunky and rich, or simple clear broths. They can contain many ingredients or few. Depending on the season, they can be used to warm us up or cool us down. The cook can create many different textures and flavors by varying the cooking methods, seasonings, ingredients, and garnishes he or she uses.

Fresh homemade soups comprise about five to ten percent of a healthful, broad-based macrobiotic diet. This averages out to about one or two cups or bowls per day. Soups are best when made daily from fresh natural ingredients. There is no comparison between fresh homemade soup and soup from a can. They are as different as night and day. Soups made in the morning or for lunch can simply be reheated and enjoyed again on the same day. Soups made in the evening can be reheated on the following day and eaten for breakfast or lunch.

Soups are not a separate category of food, as much as they are a unique way of cooking and combining foods. By adding extra water, soups are usually easier to digest than are dishes cooked with less water. Soups are often prepared with naturally fermented foods such as miso (fermented soybean paste) and shoyu (fermented soy sauce). These naturally fermented foods facilitate smooth digestion and assimilation. Soup is basic, primordial nourishment.

Because soups stimulate appetite and digestion, they are often served at the beginning of the meal. They prepare our digestive system for the rest of the meal. Ideally, the soup eaten at the beginning of the meal will complement the dishes that follow. This can be achieved by balancing the color, taste, texture, and aroma of our soups with those of our other dishes. If, for example, the other dishes are rich and hearty, a simple, clear-broth soup would make balance. If the meal is simple and light, a thick soup or stew would create harmony. Soups can also be used to balance seasonal changes. Nothing warms us up on a cold winter day like a piping hot bowl of soup. Similarly, on a hot summer day, a cool light soup helps us to cool off.

As you begin preparing healthy natural soups, try to be mindful of the following basic guidelines:

1. Select your ingredients from organic products that are naturally grown, ideally in season and from the climate or region in which you live. If organic vegetables are not available, you may temporarily substitute non-organic produce from the supermarket.

2. Try to use whole natural foods that are fresh until the time they are cooked.

3. When cutting vegetables or other foods, do them individually and place each separately so as not to mix their qualities. Try not to mix vegetables until cooking begins. Also, wipe the cutting board clean after cutting each vegetable.

4. Try to cut vegetables as elegantly and gracefully as possible so that each cut is evenly balanced.

5. As much as possible, allow foods to mix themselves during the cooking process.

6. Use seasonings moderately. Unrefined sea salt, cold-pressed vegetable oils, natural miso and shoyu, and other high-quality seasonings can be used to enhance the natural flavor of your soups. It is better to keep the taste of the seasoning mild and gentle.

7. Electric and microwave cooking are not recommended for optimal health. Among modern cooking methods, gas cooking is preferred.

8. The best quality of water for soup is clean well, spring, or mountain-stream water. City water can be used for wash-

ing foods or utensils. Distilled water is best avoided.

9. Strong spicy seasonings are not recommended in temperate climates.

10. Soups and other dishes are more appealing when beautifully and elegantly presented. The natural colors of foods can be harmonized through cooking to create colorful and attractive dishes.

11. Keep your kitchen and dining area clean and orderly. Keep the atmosphere of the dining area calm and maintain a peaceful, loving, and joyful mind while cooking.

With just these simple guidelines, plus a dash of imagination and creativity, you can cook healthful and delicious soups that are sure to please your whole family.

1
Miso Soup

Miso is the dark purée made from soybeans, sea salt, and usually barley or rice. The ingredients are first cooked and then inoculated with koji, a special mold that promotes fermentation. The mixture is placed in wooden kegs and allowed to age for a year or more. Miso is a staple food in Japan and is now recognized in Western countries for its taste, nutritional value, and important role in a healthful diet. Prompted by the demand for natural foods, several small companies have started producing high-quality natural miso in the United States.

There are a variety of uses for miso, a food that contains living enzymes that strengthen digestion, as well as a healthful balance of such nutrients as complex carbohydrates, protein, essential oils, minerals, and vitamins. Miso is most commonly used to flavor soups. Miso soups contain a variety of ingredients, including vegetables, sea vegetables, whole grains, noodles, and tofu. Miso can also be used to make pickles, and as a base for sauces, spreads, and dressings. It can sometimes be used as a seasoning in grain, bean, and vegetable dishes. Because miso is processed with sea salt, it is best used in moderate amounts. When it comes to miso, a little goes a long way.

Of the many varieties of miso available, the one I use most often is barley miso. Known in Japan as *mugi miso*, it is made from barley, soybeans, sea salt, water, and koji. The best barley miso is made from organic ingredients and naturally fermented for twenty-four to thirty-six months. This "two-year" miso is dark in color, rich in flavor, and has a mildly salty flavor. Other barley misos, known as *mellow* or *light misos*, are fermented for a shorter time. I use them as occasional supplements to two-year barley miso. Some of the other types of miso that I use are brown rice (genmai) miso, soybean (Hatcho) miso, and on occasion, white rice (kome) miso. Brown rice miso is generally lighter than barley miso, while soybean miso is usually aged for over three years and has a deep dark color and a strong rich flavor. Light, quickly fermented misos, such as white, yellow, and red miso, can occasionally be used in soups or for making dips and sauces.

Miso soup is essentially a vegetable soup to which miso is added as a seasoning. It usually includes a small amount of wakame, a nutritious sea vegetable that is an excellent source of minerals, together with a variety of vegetables that grow on land. Ingredients such as tofu, mochi (pounded sweet brown rice taffy), cooked noodles, or leftover brown rice are sometimes added. The basic method for preparing miso soup is simple. The first step is to bring the soup ingredients to a boil. The flame is then lowered and the soup is allowed to simmer for several minutes. Then miso is diluted in a little soup broth and added to the pot. The soup is then simmered, but usually not boiled, for several minutes more. Miso soup is usually garnished with freshly cut scallion, parsley, or chives.

Miso soup can be served at any meal. When you prepare it at breakfast, it is better if simply made and light in taste. Miso soup served at dinner can generally be stronger and more hearty. Miso soup is especially delicious when eaten at a meal at which brown rice is the primary grain.

Basic Miso Soup

4 to 5 cups water
1 cup onion, sliced in thin half-moons
1 to 2 inches wakame (1/4 to 1/2 inch per person),
    washed, soaked, and sliced, discard soaking water
4 tsp barley miso, puréed

2 Tbsp scallion, parsley, or chives, finely chopped, for garnish

Place the water, onion, and wakame in a pot. Cover, place over a high flame and bring to a boil. Reduce the flame to medium-low and simmer for 3 to 5 minutes. Reduce the flame to very low and wait for the water to stop boiling. Place miso in a cup or bowl, add broth, and dilute with a spoon or chopstick. Stir the diluted miso into the pot of soup. Cover and simmer for 2 to 3 minutes. Place in serving bowls and garnish with chopped scallion, parsley, or chives.

Slicing Onion in Half-Moons

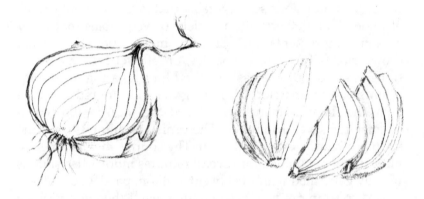

Miso Soup with Carrot, Onion, and Wakame

4 to 5 cups water
1 cup onion, sliced in thin half-moons
1/2 cup carrot, sliced in matchsticks
1 to 2 inches wakame, washed, soaked, and sliced, discard soaking water
4 tsp miso, puréed
2 Tbsp scallion, parsley, or chives, finely chopped, for garnish

Place the water and wakame in a pot. Cover, place over a high flame, and bring to a boil. Reduce flame to medium-low and simmer for about 4 to 5 minutes. Add the onion, cover, and simmer 2 to 3 minutes. Add the carrot and simmer for 2 to 3 minutes. Reduce the flame to very low and wait for the water to stop boiling. Place miso in a cup or bowl, add broth, and dilute with a spoon or chopstick. Stir the diluted miso into the pot of soup. Cover and simmer without boiling. Ladle the soup into serving bowls and garnish each with chopped scallion, parsley, or chives. Serve hot.

Slicing Carrot in Matchsticks

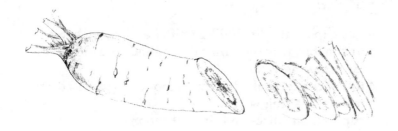

Miso Soup with Daikon, Shiitake, and Greens

4 to 5 cups water, including shiitake soaking water
1 cup daikon, sliced in thin half-moons
4 to 5 shiitake, soaked, stems removed, and sliced thin, reserve soaking water
1 to 2 inches wakame, washed, soaked, and sliced, discard soaking water
1 cup daikon greens, kale, or Chinese cabbage, sliced in 1 inch squares
1 to 2 Tbsp scallion, finely chopped, for garnish
4 tsp barley miso, puréed

Place the shiitake and water in a pot, cover, and place on a high flame. Bring to a boil, reduce the flame to medium, and simmer the shiitake for about 10 minutes. Remove the cover and add the wakame. Cover and simmer for another 3 to 4 minutes. Remove cover and add the daikon. Cover and simmer for another 2 to 3 minutes. Reduce the flame to very low so that the water stops boiling actively. Place miso in a cup or bowl, add broth, and dilute with a spoon or chopstick. Add the chopped greens and diluted miso to the pot. Cover and simmer, without boiling, for another 2 to 4 minutes. Ladle the soup into serving bowls and garnish each with scallion slices. Serve hot.

Miso Soup with Daikon and Sweet Rice Dumplings

4 to 5 cups water, including shiitake soaking water
1 to 2 inches wakame, washed, soaked, and sliced, discard soaking water
4 to 5 shiitake, soaked, stems removed, and sliced thin, reserve soaking water
1 cup daikon, sliced in thin half-moons
1 cup daikon or red radish greens, chopped thin
1/2 cup sweet brown rice or brown rice flour
1/4 cup boiling water
small pinch sea salt
4 tsp barley miso, puréed
2 Tbsp scallion or chives, finely chopped, for garnish

Place the shiitake and water in a pot and cover. Place over a high flame and bring to a boil. Reduce the flame to medium and simmer the shiitake for about 10 minutes. Add the wakame, cover, and simmer 2 to 3 minutes. Add the daikon, cover, and simmer for 2 to 3 minutes. While the shiitake and wakame are cooking, mix the rice flour with a pinch of sea salt. Add the boiling water to the flour, a little at a time, until the mixture is completely moist. Form the rice mixture into small balls, a teaspoonful at a time. With your thumb, make a shallow indentation in the center of each ball. Repeat until all the rice mixture has been formed into dumplings.

Place the dumplings in the pot with the shiitake, wakame, and daikon. Cover and simmer until the dumplings float to the surface. Reduce the flame to very low and wait for the water to stop boiling. Place miso in a cup or bowl, add broth, and dilute with a spoon or chopstick. Add the daikon greens and diluted miso. Cover and simmer, without boiling, for 2 to 3 minutes. Ladle the soup and dumplings into serving bowls and garnish with chopped scallion or chives.

Slicing Daikon in Half-Moons

Miso Soup with Daikon, Celery, and Tofu

4 to 5 cups water
1 to 2 inches wakame, washed, soaked, and sliced, discard soaking water
1 cup daikon, sliced in thin rectangles or matchsticks
1/2 cup celery, sliced on a thin diagonal
1/2 cup daikon or red radish greens, sliced in 1 inch lengths
1/2 cup tofu, sliced in small cubes
4 tsp miso, puréed
2 Tbsp scallion, finely chopped, for garnish

Place the water and wakame in a pot. Cover, place over a high flame, and bring to a boil. Reduce the flame to medium-low and simmer for 2 to 3 minutes. Add the daikon and celery, cover, and simmer for 3 to 4 minutes. Add the tofu and reduce the flame to very low. Wait for the water to stop boiling. Place miso in a cup or bowl, add broth, and dilute with a spoon or chopstick. Add the greens and puréed miso to the pot. Simmer, without boiling, for another 2 to 3 minutes. Ladle into soup bowls and garnish with chopped scallion.

Miso Soup with Daikon and Lotus Root Dumplings

4 to 5 cups water, including shiitake soaking water
1 cup daikon, sliced in thin quarter-moons
4 to 5 shiitake, soaked, stems removed, and sliced thin, reserve soaking water
1 to 2 inches wakame, washed, soaked, and sliced, discard soaking water
1/2 cup fresh lotus root, finely grated
unbleached white or whole wheat pastry flour
1 tsp fresh ginger juice
small pinch sea salt
1/2 cup Chinese cabbage, sliced in 1 inch squares
4 tsp miso, puréed
2 Tbsp scallion or chives, finely chopped, for garnish

Place the water and shiitake in a pot. Cover, place over a high flame, and bring to a boil. Reduce the flame to medium-low and simmer for about 10 minutes. Add the wakame, cover, and simmer 3 to 4 minutes. While the shiitake and wakame are simmering, place the grated lotus root, sea salt, and ginger juice in a mixing bowl. Add enough flour to the mixture to form a moist but loose dough, mixing thoroughly. Take a teaspoonful of the lotus mixture and roll into a small ball. Repeat until all the lotus mixture is used up. Place a shallow indentation in the center of each ball with your thumb.

Place the dumplings in the hot soup, cover, and simmer until the balls float to the surface. Reduce the flame to very low and wait for the water to stop boiling. Place the Chinese cabbage in the pot. Place miso in a cup or bowl, add broth, and dilute with a spoon or chopstick. Add to the soup. Cover and simmer, without boiling, for 2 to 3 minutes. Place in serving bowls and garnish with chopped scallion.

Sweet Summer Miso Soup

4 to 5 cups water
1 to 2 inches wakame, washed, soaked, and sliced, discard soaking water
1/2 cup onion, sliced in thin half-moons
1/4 cup carrot, sliced in thin matchsticks
1/4 cup sweet corn, removed from cob
1/4 cup buttercup, butternut, or other winter squash, cubed
1/4 cup cabbage, sliced in 1 inch squares
4 tsp miso, puréed
2 Tbsp scallion, parsley, or chives, finely chopped, for garnish

Place the water in a pot, cover, and bring to a boil. Add the wakame, cover, and reduce the flame to medium-low. Simmer for 2 to 3 minutes. Add the onion, cover, and simmer for 1 to 2 minutes. Add the corn, squash, and cabbage. Cover and simmer for another 2 to 3 minutes. Reduce the flame to very low and wait for the water to stop boiling. Place miso in a cup or bowl, add broth, and dilute with a spoon or chopstick. Add the puréed miso and simmer, without boiling, for another 2 to 3 minutes. Place in serving bowls and garnish each with chopped scallion, parsley, or chives.

Cutting Squash in Cubes

Hearty Winter Miso Soup

    4 to 5 cups water
    1/2 cup onion, sliced in thin half-moons
    1/4 cup carrot, sliced in thin matchsticks
    1/4 cup buttercup, butternut, or other winter squash,
      cubed
    1/8 cup burdock, sliced in matchsticks
    1/8 cup cabbage, sliced in 1 inch squares
    1/8 cup wakame, washed, soaked, and sliced, discard
      soaking water
    light or dark sesame oil
    4 tsp miso, puréed
    2 Tbsp scallion, finely chopped, for garnish

    Place a small amount of sesame oil in a pot and heat. Add the onion and sauté for 2 to 3 minutes. Add the burdock and sauté for another 2 to 3 minutes. Add the carrot, squash, cabbage, and wakame. Sauté for 1 to 2 minutes. Add the water, cover, and bring to a boil. Reduce the flame to medium-low and simmer for another 5 to 7 minutes. Reduce the flame to very low and wait for the water to stop boiling. Place miso in a cup or bowl, add broth, and dilute with a spoon or chopstick. Add the puréed miso, cover, and simmer, without boiling, for another 2 to 3 minutes. Place in serving bowls and garnish each with chopped scallion, parsley, or chives.

Miso Soup with Sweet Corn

    4 to 5 cups water
    1 cup sweet corn, removed from cob
    1/8 cup celery, diced
    1/2 cup onion, diced
    1/4 cup green string beans, chopped in 1 inch lengths
    1/4 cup snow peas, stems removed
    1 sheet nori, toasted and sliced in thin strips (2 to 3
      inches long)

4 tsp miso, puréed
2 Tbsp scallion, finely chopped, for garnish

Place the water in a pot, cover, and bring to a boil. Add the onion, cover, and simmer for 2 to 3 minutes. Add the celery, sweet corn, and green beans. Cover and reduce the flame to medium-low. Simmer for about 3 to 4 minutes. Reduce the flame to very low and wait for the water to stop boiling. Place miso in a cup or bowl, add broth, and dilute with a spoon or chopstick. Add the puréed miso and snow peas. Cover and simmer 2 to 3 minutes. Place in serving bowls and garnish each with chopped scallion.

Quick One-Cup Miso Soup

1 cup water
1 sheet nori, toasted and torn into 1 inch pieces
1/4 cup scallion, finely chopped
1/2 to 1 tsp miso, puréed

Place water in a saucepan, cover, and bring to a boil. Reduce the flame to very low and wait for the water to stop boiling. Place miso in a cup or bowl, add broth, and dilute with a spoon or chopstick. Add the puréed miso, scallion, and nori. Cover and simmer, without boiling, for 2 to 3 minutes. Place in serving bowl.

Quick Miso Soup with Tofu and Nori

4 to 5 cups water
1 cup tofu, sliced in small cubes or diced
2 sheets nori, toasted and cut in thin strips or torn into 1 inch pieces
4 tsp miso, puréed
1/4 cup scallion, finely chopped

Place water in a pot, cover, and bring to a boil. Reduce

the flame to very low and wait for the water to stop boiling. Place miso in a cup or bowl, add broth, and dilute with a spoon or chopstick. Add the tofu and puréed miso. Cover and simmer, without boiling, for 2 to 3 minutes. Add the nori and scallion. Place in serving bowls.

Quick Miso Soup with Natto

4 to 5 cup water
1 cup daikon, sliced in thin quarter-moons
2 sheets nori, toasted and torn into 1 inch pieces
1/2 cup natto (whole fermented soybeans)
1/4 cup scallion, finely chopped
4 tsp barley miso, puréed

Place the water and daikon in a pot. Cover and bring to a boil. Reduce the flame to very low and simmer for 2 minutes. Place miso in a cup or bowl, add broth, and dilute with a spoon or chopstick. Add the miso, natto, nori, and scallion. Simmer, without boiling, for 2 to 3 minutes. Place in serving bowls.

French Onion Miso Soup

4 to 5 cups water, including shiitake and kombu soak-
     ing water
2 cups onion, sliced in thin half-moons
4 to 5 shiitake, soaked, stems removed, and thinly
     sliced, reserve soaking water
1 strip kombu, 2 to 3 inches long, soaked and sliced in
     thin matchsticks, reserve soaking water
1/2 cup whole wheat or sourdough bread cubes, for gar-
     nish
2 Tbsp scallion, finely chopped, for garnish
1 1/2 to 2 1/2 Tbsp miso, puréed
light or dark sesame oil

Place the onion, shiitake, and kombu in a pot. Add the

water, cover, and bring to a boil. Reduce the flame to medi-um-low and simmer for 15 to 20 minutes until the shiitake are tender. Reduce the flame to very low. Place miso in a cup or bowl, add broth, and dilute with a spoon or chopstick. Add the diluted miso and simmer, without boiling, for 2 to 3 min-utes. While the soup is simmering, brush a small amount of oil in a skillet and heat. Add the bread cubes and sauté for 3 to 4 minutes until slightly crisp and browned. Place the soup in serving bowls and garnish with several roasted bread cubes and a small amount of chopped scallion.

Miso Soup with Mochi

4 to 5 cups water
1 cup onion, sliced in thin half-moons
1/2 cup carrot, sliced in matchsticks
1/4 cup cabbage, thinly sliced
1 to 2 inches wakame, washed, soaked, and sliced
8 to 10 pieces mochi (pounded rice taffy), 2 inches by 3 inches
1 1/2 to 2 1/2 Tbsp miso, puréed
2 Tbsp scallion, chives, parsley, or watercress, finely chopped, for garnish

Place the water in a pot, cover, and bring to a boil. Add the wakame, cover, and simmer 2 to 3 minutes. Add the on-ion, carrot, and cabbage. Cover and simmer for 3 to 4 min-utes. Heat a skillet and place the mochi squares in it. Cover the skillet and reduce the flame to low in order to brown the mochi. When slightly brown, turn the mochi over and brown the other side. The mochi should puff up slightly. Remove the mochi and place 2 pieces in each soup bowl. Reduce the flame under the soup until it stops boiling. Place miso in a cup or bowl, add broth, and dilute with a spoon or chopstick. Add the diluted miso and simmer for 2 to 3 minutes. Ladle the soup over the mochi and garnish each bowl with the chopped greens.

Ozoni (Japanese New Year Miso Soup)

    4 to 5 cups water
    4 to 5 daikon rounds, 1/4 inch thick
    4 to 5 small taro (albi) potatoes, peeled and quartered
    8 to 10 pieces mochi, 2 inches by 3 inches, pan-toasted
    1 1/2 to 2 1/2 Tbsp white or yellow miso, puréed
    4 to 5 sprigs watercress
    1 strip kombu, 2 to 3 inches long, rinsed
    1/2 sheet nori, toasted and cut in thin strips, for garnish
    2 Tbsp scallion, finely chopped, for garnish

Place the kombu, daikon, and taro in a pot. Add the water, cover, and bring to a boil. Reduce the flame to medium-low and simmer for 4 to 5 minutes. Remove the kombu and set aside. You may use it in other dishes. Cover the pot and continue to simmer for another 10 minutes or until the daikon and taro are tender. Reduce the flame to very low until the water stops boiling. Place miso in a cup or bowl, add broth, and dilute with a spoon or chopstick. Add the puréed miso and simmer, without boiling, for 2 to 3 minutes. Place 2 pieces of mochi in each serving bowl. Ladle the soup over the mochi and place a sprig of watercress in each bowl. Garnish with several strips of nori and chopped scallion.

Miso Soup with Winter Squash and Dulse

    4 to 5 cups water
    2 cups uncooked winter squash skins, sliced in thin
      matchsticks
    1/2 cup leek, sliced in thin rounds
    1 1/2 to 2 1/2 Tbsp miso, puréed
    1/4 cup dulse (1/2 oz dry), washed, soaked, and sliced
    2 Tbsp scallion, finely chopped, for garnish

Place the water in a pot, cover, and bring to a boil. Add the dulse and squash skins. Cover and simmer for 2 to 3 minutes. Reduce the flame to very low until the water stops boiling. Place miso in a cup or bowl, add broth, and dilute with a spoon or chopstick. Add the leek and puréed miso. Simmer, without boiling, for 2 to 3 minutes. Place in soup bowls and garnish with chopped scallion.

Puréed Squash Soup with Miso

4 to 5 cup water
1 medium buttercup squash, skin removed and sliced
   into cubes
1 to 2 inches wakame, washed, soaked, and sliced
1/2 cup onion, finely diced
1 1/2 to 2 1/2 Tbsp miso, puréed
2 Tbsp scallion, chives, or parsley, finely chopped, for
   garnish
water, for cooking squash

Place the squash in a pot. Add enough water to cover the squash. Cover and bring to a boil. Reduce the flame to medium-low and simmer for 7 to 10 minutes until the squash is tender. Pureé the squash and cooking water in a hand food mill. Place the purée back in the pot, and add the onion and wakame. Cover and bring to a boil again. Reduce the flame to very low and simmer for 3 to 4 minutes. Place miso in a cup or bowl, add broth, and dilute with a spoon or chopstick. Add the puréed miso and simmer, without boiling, for another 2 to 3 minutes. Place in serving bowls and garnish with the chopped scallion.

Hand Food Mill

Miso Soup with Broccoli and Fu

4 to 5 cups water
1 to 2 inches wakame, washed, soaked, and sliced
1/2 cup onion, sliced in thin half-moons
1 to 1 1/2 cups broccoli flowerets
1/4 cup carrot, sliced in thin matchsticks
4 rounds of fu (puffed wheat gluten), soaked 10 minutes and sliced in bite-sized pieces
1 1/2 to 2 1/2 Tbsp miso, puréed
2 Tbsp parsley, finely chopped, for garnish

Place the water and fu in a pot. Cover and bring to a boil. Reduce the flame to medium-low and simmer for 4 to 5 minutes. Add the wakame and simmer for 2 to 3 minutes. Add the onion and broccoli and simmer for another 2 to 3 minutes. Place miso in a cup or bowl, add broth, and dilute with a spoon or chopstick. Reduce the flame to very low and add the puréed miso. Simmer, without boiling, for 2 to 3 minutes. Place in serving bowls and garnish with chopped parsley.

Millet and Squash Soup with Miso

4 to 5 cups water
1/4 cup millet, washed
1 cup buttercup, butternut, or other winter squash, sliced in 1/2 to 1 inch pieces
1/4 cup onion, diced
1/4 cup celery, diced
2 Tbsp burdock, diced
1 strip kombu, 2 inches long, soaked and diced
1 1/2 to 2 1/2 Tbsp miso, puréed
2 Tbsp parsley or chives, finely chopped, for garnish

Place the kombu, onion, celery, squash, and burdock in a pot. Add the water, cover, and bring to a boil. Reduce the flame to medium-low and simmer for 30 to 35 minutes. Place miso in a cup or bowl, add broth, and dilute with a spoon or chopstick. Reduce the flame to very low and add the puréed miso. Simmer, without boiling, for 2 to 3 minutes. Place in serving bowls and garnish.

Quick Grain Miso Soup

   4 to 5 cups water
   1 cup leftover cooked millet, rice, or barley
   1/4 cup onion, diced
   1 cup buttercup, butternut, gold nugget, red kuri, delic-
      ata, or other winter squash, sliced in 1/2 inch cubes
   1/4 cup celery, diced
   1/4 cup green peas or green beans, sliced in 1 inch
      lengths
   1 1/2 to 2 1/2 Tbsp miso, puréed
   1 sheet toasted nori, cut in thin strips, for garnish
   2 Tbsp scallion, finely chopped, for garnish

Place the water, leftover grain, onion, squash, celery, and green peas or green beans in a pot. Cover and bring to a boil. Reduce the flame to medium-low and simmer for 15 to 20 minutes until the grain is soft. Place miso in a cup or bowl, add broth, and dilute with a spoon or chopstick. Reduce the flame to very low. Add the miso and simmer, without boiling, for 2 to 3 minutes. Place in serving bowls and garnish with chopped scallion.

Quick Noodle or Pasta Miso Soup

   4 to 5 cups water, including shiitake soaking water
   1 lb udon, somen, soba, or other pasta, cooked
   1 to 2 inches wakame, washed, soaked, and sliced
   4 to 5 shiitake, soaked, stems removed, and diced,
      reserve soaking water
   1 cup Chinese cabbage, sliced thin
   1/2 cup tofu, diced in 1/4 inch cubes

1 1/2 to 2 1/2 Tbsp miso, puréed
2 Tbsp scallion, finely chopped, for garnish

Place the shiitake, wakame, and water in a pot. Cover and bring to a boil. Reduce the flame to medium-low and simmer for 7 to 10 minutes. Reduce the flame to very low. Place miso in a cup or bowl, add broth, and dilute with a spoon or chopstick. Add the cooked noodles or pasta, Chinese cabbage, tofu, and puréed miso. Simmer, without boiling, for 2 to 3 minutes. Place in serving bowls and garnish with chopped scallion.

Miso Soup with Natto and Grated Daikon

4 to 5 cups water
1 1/2 cups daikon, finely grated
1 cup natto
1 1/2 to 2 1/2 Tbsp miso, puréed
1 sheet toasted nori, cut in thin strips, for garnish
1/4 cup scallion, finely chopped, for garnish

Place water in a pot, cover, and bring to a boil. Reduce the flame to medium-low and simmer for 2 to 3 minutes. Reduce the flame to very low. Place miso in a cup or bowl, add broth, and dilute with a spoon or chopstick. Add the natto and puréed miso. Simmer, without boiling, for 2 to 3 minutes. Place in serving bowls and garnish with several strips of nori and a teaspoon or so of sliced scallion.

White Miso Soup with Noodles and Croutons

1 package (8 oz) somen (thin wheat noodles), cooked
1 cup bread cubes, for making croutons
4 to 5 cups water, including shiitake and kombu soaking water
2 cups onion, sliced in thin half-moons
1 strip kombu, 2 to 3 inches long, soaked and finely

minced, reserve soaking water
4 to 5 shiitake, soaked, stems removed, and diced, reserve soaking water
1/2 cup carrot, sliced in thin matchsticks
1 1/2 to 2 1/2 Tbsp miso, puréed
1/4 cup parsley, minced, for garnish
light sesame oil, for deep-frying croutons

Place the kombu, shiitake, and onion in a pot. Add the water, cover, and bring to a boil. Reduce the flame to medium-low and simmer for 10 minutes until the shiitake and kombu are tender. Reduce the flame to very low. Place miso in a cup or bowl, add broth, and dilute with a spoon or chopstick. Add the carrot, cooked somen, and puréed miso. Simmer, without boiling, for 2 to 3 minutes. Heat 2 inches of oil in a deep-frying pot. Deep-fry the bread cubes until golden brown. Remove and drain on paper towels. Place the soup in serving bowls and garnish with croutons and chopped parsley.

2
Hearty Grain Soups

Whole grains are incredibly versatile foods. When cooked by themselves or in combination, whole grains can serve as the main dish in a meal. They can also be cooked with beans, vegetables, sea vegetables, and other healthful ingredients to create an array of nutritious and appetizing entrees. Whole grains are also delicious when prepared in soups. Whole grain soups are a meal in themselves. They can range from thick and creamy barley, millet, and rice and vegetable stews to clear shoyu broths with brown rice and vegetables. Whole grains can also be used as a base for a variety of creamy vegetable soups. Whole grain soups complement your other natural food dishes and help create nutritious balance in your meal.

Quick Brown Rice Soup

> 4 to 5 cups water, including shiitake soaking water
> 2 cups leftover cooked brown rice
> 1/4 cup scallion, thinly sliced
> 4 shiitake, soaked, stems removed, and quartered, reserve soaking water
> 2 sheets toasted nori, cut in squares or strips
> 2 to 3 Tbsp shoyu

Place the shiitake and water in a pot, cover, and bring to a boil. Reduce the flame to medium-low and simmer 10 minutes. Reduce the flame to low. Add the cooked brown rice and shoyu. Cover and simmer 4 to 5 minutes. Add the scallion and nori. Place in serving bowls.

Brown Rice and Pumpkin Soup

4 to 5 cups water
2 cups leftover cooked brown rice
1 cup Hokkaido pumpkin or other winter squash,
   sliced in 1/2 inch chunks
1/2 cup onion, diced
2 Tbsp scallion or parsley, finely chopped, for garnish
1/4 to 1/3 tsp sea salt

Place the onion, pumpkin or squash, and cooked brown rice in a pot. Add water, cover, and bring to a boil. Reduce the flame to medium-low and simmer for 15 to 20 minutes until creamy. Add the sea salt, cover, and simmer another 10 minutes. Place in serving bowls and garnish with chopped scallion or parsley.

Brown Rice and Azuki Bean Soup

1/2 cup brown rice, washed
1/4 cup azuki beans, washed and soaked 6 to 8 hours or
   overnight, reserve soaking water
5 cups water, including azuki bean, kombu, and shiitake soaking water
1 strip kombu, 1 inch long, soaked and diced, reserve
   soaking water
1 cup daikon, diced
4 to 5 shiitake, soaked, stems removed, and diced, reserve soaking water
1/4 to 1/2 tsp sea salt
1/4 to 1/3 cup scallion, finely chopped, for garnish

Place the rice, azuki beans, kombu, shiitake, and water in a pressure cooker. Cover and bring up to pressure over a high flame. Reduce the flame to medium-low and simmer for 45 to 50 minutes. Remove from the flame and let the pressure come down. Remove the cover and add the daikon and sea salt. Cover with a regular lid (not the pressure cooker lid) and bring to a boil. Reduce the flame to medium-low and simmer for 10 to 15 minutes. Add the chopped scallion and simmer 1 minute. Place in serving bowls.

White Rice and Deep-Fried Tofu Soup

4 to 5 cups water
1 cup organic white sushi rice, washed
1/2 lb firm style tofu, sliced in 1/4 to 1/2 inch thick
  slices
1/2 cup onion, diced
1/4 cup celery, diced
1/4 cup carrot, diced
1/2 cup green peas, removed from pod
light sesame oil, for deep-frying tofu
1/4 to 1/2 tsp sea salt
1/4 cup scallion, finely sliced, for garnish
1 sheet toasted nori, cut in thin strips, for garnish

Place the onion, celery, carrot, green peas, and white rice in a pot. Cover and bring to a boil. Reduce the flame to medium-low and simmer for 20 to 30 minutes. While the soup is cooking, heat 2 to 3 inches of sesame oil in a deep-frying pot. Deep-fry the tofu until golden. Remove and drain on paper towels. Slice the tofu into small cubes or thin strips. Place the tofu in the pot with the rice and vegetables. Add the sea salt, cover, and cook for another 10 minutes. Place in serving bowls and garnish with scallion and several strips of nori.

Ten-don (White Rice in Broth with Tempura)

Ten-don is a very rich, delicious, and satisfying dish, particularly in cold weather. The results are well worth the effort.

Rice
2 cups organic white sushi rice, washed
2 cups water, for cooking rice
pinch of sea salt, for rice

Broth
4 to 5 cups water, including shiitake and kombu soaking water
1 strip kombu, 2 inches long, soaked, reserve soaking water
4 shiitake, soaked and stems removed, reserve soaking water
2 to 3 tsp shoyu, for broth
2 Tbsp bonito (dried fish) flakes (can be omitted)
2 tsp fresh ginger juice

Tempura
1 cup green beans, stems removed and sliced in half lengthwise
1 cup carrot, sliced in matchsticks
1/4 cup onion, sliced in thin half-moons
2 Tbsp burdock, sliced in thin matchsticks
light sesame oil, for deep-frying tempura
3/4 cup whole wheat pastry flour
1/4 cup corn flour
1 Tbsp kuzu, diluted in 2 Tbsp water
1/8 tsp sea salt
1 to 1 1/4 cup natural sparkling water, for tempura batter
1/4 cup scallion, finely sliced, for garnish

To prepare the rice: Place the white rice, water, and sea salt in a pressure cooker. Cover and bring up to pressure over a high flame. Reduce the flame to low and place a flame deflector under the cooker. Cook for 20 minutes. Remove from the flame and allow the pressure to come down. Remove the cover. Place 1/2 to 1/3 cup cooked rice in serving bowls.

To prepare the broth: Place the kombu, shiitake, bonito flakes, and water in a pot. Cover and bring to a boil. Reduce the flame to medium-low and simmer for 5 minutes. Remove the kombu and set aside. You may use it in other dishes. Let the broth simmer for another 10 minutes and then remove the shiitake. You may use in other dishes or quarter it and place it back in the broth. Reduce the flame to low, add the shoyu, and simmer another 5 minutes. Add the ginger juice just before serving.

To prepare the tempura batter: Combine the flours and sea salt. Mix thoroughly. Add the diluted kuzu and sparkling water. Mix thoroughly to remove any lumps. Place the batter in the freezer for 10 to 15 minutes to chill. Remove the batter. Heat 2 to 3 inches of oil in a deep-frying pot. Place the green beans, onion, carrot, and burdock in the batter. When the oil is hot, take a tablespoonful of the vegetables in batter and place in the hot oil. Place 4 to 5 more tablespoonfuls in the oil. Deep-fry until golden brown. Remove and drain on paper towels. Repeat until all tempura is cooked.

Place 2 to 3 pieces of tempura on top of each serving of white rice. Ladle the hot broth over each serving of rice and tempura to just cover the rice. Garnish and serve.

White Rice and Green Tea Soup

2 cups leftover cooked organic white rice
4 to 5 cups water
4 to 5 tsp green tea leaves
1 medium to large umeboshi plum
1/2 sheet toasted nori, cut in thin strips, for garnish
2 Tbsp scallion, finely chopped, for garnish

Place the water in a pot, cover, and bring almost to a boil. Add the tea leaves. Do not boil. Turn off the flame, cover the pot, and let steep for one minute only. Place the rice in serving bowls while the tea is being prepared. Pull the umeboshi plum apart and place an equal amount on top of each serving of rice. Pour the hot tea over the rice, while straining the leaves with a tea strainer. Garnish each bowl with several strips of nori and chopped scallion.

Cream of Celery Soup

2 cups leftover cooked brown rice
4 to 5 cups water
2 cups celery, finely diced
1/2 cup onion, finely diced
2 Tbsp corn oil
1/4 to 1/2 tsp sea salt
2 Tbsp scallion, parsley, or chives, finely chopped, for garnish

Place the cooked brown rice and water in a pot. Cover and bring to a boil. Reduce the flame to medium-low and simmer for 20 minutes until very soft and creamy. Remove from the flame. Place all of the rice and cooking water in a hand food mill and purée until smooth and creamy. Place the purée back in the pot. Cover and bring to a boil. While the rice is cooking, heat the corn oil in a skillet. Sauté the onion for 1 to 2 minutes. Add the celery and sauté another 3 to 5 minutes. Place the sautéed vegetables in the pot with the puréed rice. Cover and simmer 5 to 7 minutes. Add the sea salt and simmer until the vegetables are soft (about 10 to 15 minutes). Place in serving bowls and garnish.

Cream of Mushroom Soup

2 cups leftover cooked brown rice
1/4 cup rolled oats
5 cups water
3 cups fresh mushrooms, sliced thin or diced
1/2 cup onion, finely diced

2 Tbsp corn oil
2 to 3 tsp shoyu
2 Tbsp scallion, parsley, or chives, finely chopped, for
   garnish

Place the rice, rolled oats, and water in a pot. Cover and bring to a boil. Reduce the flame to medium-low and simmer for 15 to 20 minutes. Remove and purée the grain and liquid in a hand food mill until creamy. Return to the cooking pot. Cover and bring to a boil. While the grain is cooking, heat the oil in a skillet. Add the onion and sauté 1 to 2 minutes. Add the mushrooms and a few drops of shoyu. Sauté for 5 minutes. Remove and place in the pot with the puréed grain. Cover and bring to a boil. Reduce the flame to medium-low and simmer for another 20 minutes until the vegetables are soft. Season with the remaining shoyu and simmer for another 5 minutes. Place in serving bowls and garnish.

Millet and Squash Soup

1/2 cup millet, washed
4 to 5 cups water
1 square inch kombu, soaked and diced
1/2 cup onion, diced
1 cup buttercup or butternut squash, cubed or diced
1/4 cup celery, diced
1/4 cup carrot, diced
1/2 cup leek, sliced thin
1/4 to 1/2 tsp sea salt
2 Tbsp parsley, finely chopped, for garnish

Place the kombu, onion, celery, squash, and carrot in a pot. Add the millet and water. Cover and bring to a boil. Reduce the flame to medium-low and simmer for 25 to 30 minutes. Add the sea salt and cook another 10 minutes. Add the leek and simmer another 2 to 3 minutes. Place in serving bowls and garnish.

Millet and Corn Soup

4 to 5 cups water
1/2 cup millet, washed
1 cup sweet corn, removed from cob
1/4 cup onion, finely minced
1/4 to 1/2 tsp sea salt
2 Tbsp parsley, finely minced, for garnish
1 sheet toasted nori, cut in thin strips, for garnish

Place the millet and water in a pot. Cover and bring to a boil. Reduce the flame to medium-low and simmer for 25 to 30 minutes. Add the sweet corn, onion, and sea salt. Cover and cook another 10 minutes. Place in serving bowls and garnish with parsley and several strips of nori.

Hato Mugi Soup

4 to 5 cups water, including kombu, hato mugi, dried daikon, and shiitake soaking water
1 cup hato mugi (pearl barley), soaked 3 to 4 hours, reserve soaking water
1 strip kombu, 2 to 3 inches long, soaked, reserve soaking water
4 to 5 shiitake, soaked, stems removed, and diced, reserve soaking water
1/2 cup onion, diced
1/4 cup celery, diced
1/4 cup carrot, diced
1/2 cup sweet corn, removed from cob
2 Tbsp dried daikon, washed, soaked, and sliced, reserve soaking water
3 to 4 pieces dried tofu, soaked and diced, discard soaking water
1/4 cup buttercup or butternut squash, diced
1/4 cup leek, finely chopped
1/4 to 1/2 tsp sea salt

1 Tbsp parsley, minced, for garnish

Place the hato mugi, kombu, shiitake, and dried daikon in a pressure cooker. Add water, place the lid on the cooker, and bring up to pressure over a high flame. Reduce the flame to medium-low and cook for 20 minutes. Remove from the flame and let the pressure come down. Remove the lid. Add the onion, celery, carrot, dried tofu, and squash. Cover the cooker with a lid (not the pressure cooker lid). Bring to a boil. Add the sea salt and reduce the flame to medium-low. Simmer for another 20 to 25 minutes until the vegetables and hato mugi are tender. Add the leek and simmer another 3 to 5 minutes. Place in serving bowls and garnish with chopped parsley.

Barley Mushroom Soup

1/2 cup partially pearled barley, soaked 3 to 4 hours, reserve soaking water
4 to 5 cups water, including barley soaking water
1 cup mushroom, diced
1/2 cup onion, diced
1/4 cup celery or celery root, diced
1/4 cup carrot, diced
1/4 cup rutabaga, diced
1/2 cup tofu, cubed and deep-fried until golden (can be omitted)
2 Tbsp shoyu
2 Tbsp scallion, finely chopped, for garnish

Place the barley and water in a pressure cooker, cover, and bring up to pressure over a high flame. Reduce the flame to medium-low and cook for 35 minutes. Remove from the flame and let the pressure come down. Remove the cover. Place the cooker over a high flame. Add the onion, mushrooms, celery, carrot, rutabaga, and fried tofu. Cover with a lid (not the pressure cooker lid). Bring to a boil again. Reduce the flame to medium-low and simmer for another 10 to 15 minutes. Add the shoyu, cover, and simmer another 5 minutes. Place in serving bowls and garnish with chopped scallion.

Barley Lentil Soup

> 4 to 5 cups water, including barley soaking water
> 1/2 cup partially pearled barley, soaked 3 to 4 hours, reserve soaking water
> 1/4 cup brown or green lentils, washed
> 1/2 cup onion, diced
> 1/4 cup celery, diced
> 1/4 cup carrot, diced
> 1/2 cup leek, chopped in 1/4 to 1/2 inch-long pieces
> 1/4 to 1/2 tsp sea salt
> 2 Tbsp parsley, minced, for garnish

Place the water, lentils, and barley in a pot. Cover and bring to a boil. Reduce the flame to medium-low and simmer for 30 minutes. Add the onion, celery, and carrot. Cover and simmer another 5 minutes. Add the sea salt, cover, and simmer 10 minutes. Add the leek, cover, and simmer another 2 to 3 minutes. Place in serving bowls and garnish with chopped parsley.

Seitan Barley Stew

> 1/2 cup partially pearled barley, soaked 4 hours
> 5 cups water, including barley, shiitake, and kombu soaking water
> 4 to 5 shiitake mushrooms, soaked, stems removed, and diced
> 1 strip kombu, 2 inches long, soaked and diced
> 1/4 cup onion, diced
> 1/4 cup carrot, diced
> 1 cup cooked seitan, diced
> 1/4 cup leeks, sliced in thin rounds

1/4 cup celery, diced
1/8 cup green string beans or yellow wax beans, sliced
   in 1 inch lengths
2 to 3 Tbsp shoyu
1/4 cup scallion, chives, or parsley, finely chopped, for
   garnish

Place the barley, kombu, shiitake, and water in a pot.
Cover and bring to a boil. Reduce the flame to medium-low
and simmer about 45 minutes until the barley is tender. Add
the onion, carrot, seitan, celery, and green or yellow beans.
Simmer for 2 to 3 minutes. Add the shoyu and leek. Cover
and simmer another 4 to 5 minutes. Place in serving bowls
and garnish.

Corn Chowder

4 to 5 cups water
1/2 cup yellow corn grits
2 cups corn, removed from cob
1/2 cups onion, diced
1/4 cup celery, diced
1/4 to 1/2 tsp sea salt
2 Tbsp parsley, finely minced, for garnish

Place the water in a pot, cover, and bring to a boil. Slowly
pour the grits into the boiling water, stirring constantly with a
wire whisk to prevent lumping, until the water comes to a
boil again. Add the corn, onion, and celery. Reduce the flame
to medium-low and simmer 2 to 3 minutes. Add the sea salt,
cover, and simmer another 15 to 20 minutes until the grits are
done. Place in serving bowls and garnish with minced parsley.

Kasha Vegetable Soup

4 to 5 cups water
1 cup roasted buckwheat (kasha)
1 cup onion, diced
1/4 cup celery, diced
1/4 cup cabbage, diced
1/4 cup sauerkraut, chopped
1/4 to 1/2 tsp sea salt
1/4 cup parsley, minced

Place the water in a pot, cover, and bring to a boil. Add
the buckwheat, onion, celery, cabbage, and sauerkraut. Cover
and bring to a boil. Reduce the flame to medium-low and
simmer for 10 minutes. Add the sea salt, cover, and simmer
another 10 minutes. Mix in the parsley and place in serving
bowls.

White Rice Soup with Summer Vegetables

4 to 5 cups water
1/4 cup organic white rice
1/4 cup onion, diced
1/4 cup celery, diced
1/4 cup carrot, diced
1/4 cup green peas, removed from pod
1/4 cup green beans, stems removed and sliced in 1/2
  inch lengths
1/4 cup yellow wax beans, stems removed and sliced in
  1/2 inch lengths
1/2 cup sweet corn, removed from cob
1/4 cup fresh lima beans
2 to 3 tsp umeboshi paste or 2 to 2 1/2 Tbsp umeboshi
  vinegar
2 Tbsp chives, minced, for garnish

Place the water, white rice, onion, celery, carrot, peas,

string beans, corn, and lima beans in a pot. Cover and bring to a boil. Reduce the flame to medium-low and simmer for 20 minutes or until the rice and vegetables are tender. Add the umeboshi paste or vinegar, stir well, cover, and simmer another 5 minutes. Serve in bowls and garnish with chives.

Oat Soup with Dulse

4 to 5 cups water
1 to 1 1/2 cups rolled oats
1/2 cup onion, diced
1 cup broccoli, flowerets
1/4 cup dulse, washed, soaked 3 minutes, and chopped, discard soaking water
1/4 to 1/2 tsp sea salt
2 Tbsp scallion, finely chopped, for garnish

Place the water in a pot, cover, and bring to a boil. Add the rolled oats and stir constantly until the water comes to a boil again. Add the onion, reduce the flame to medium-low, cover, and simmer 5 minutes. Add the sea salt, cover, and simmer another 7 minutes. Add the broccoli, cover, and simmer another 3 minutes. Add the dulse and simmer 1 to 2 more minutes. Place in serving bowls and garnish.

French Onion Soup with Mochi

4 to 5 cups water, including kombu and shiitake soaking water
2 cups onion, sliced in thin half-moons
5 shiitake, soaked, stems removed, and diced, reserve soaking water
1 strip kombu, 2 inches long, soaked and diced, reserve soaking water
2 tsp corn oil
1/4 cup bonito flakes
2 cups whole wheat bread cubes, pan-roasted until

golden
1 cup mochi, sliced in 1/2 inch cubes, pan-roasted
2 to 3 Tbsp shoyu
2 Tbsp scallion or chives, finely chopped, for garnish

Heat the corn oil in a pot. Sauté the onion for 3 to 5 minutes. Add the water, kombu, shiitake, and bonito flakes. Cover and bring to a boil. Reduce the flame to medium-low and simmer for 20 minutes until the onion, kombu, and shiitake are tender. Add the shoyu, cover, and simmer another 5 minutes. Place in serving bowls and garnish with toasted mochi, bread croutons, and chopped scallion or chives. This soup may be baked in the oven like traditional French onion soup until the mochi resembles melted cheese.

Sweet Rice and Vegetable Soup

4 to 5 cups water, including shiitake soaking water
1/2 to 3/4 cup sweet brown rice
1/2 cup onion, diced
1/4 cup celery, diced
1/4 cup carrot, sliced in matchsticks
2 Tbsp burdock, diced
5 shiitake, soaked, stems removed, and diced, reserve
  soaking water
1/2 sheet toasted nori, cut in thin strips, for garnish
2 Tbsp scallion, finely chopped, for garnish

Place the sweet rice and water in a pot, cover, and bring to a boil. Reduce the flame to medium-low and simmer for 50 minutes. Puree' the rice and liquid in a hand food mill. Place back in the pot. Add the shiitake, onion, celery, carrot, and burdock. Cover and bring to a boil again. Reduce the flame to medium-low and add the sea salt. Cover and simmer another 15 minutes, until the shiitake are tender. Place in serving bowls and garnish with chopped scallion and several strips of toasted nori.

Fu and Broth

4 to 5 cups water, including kombu, shiitake, and fu
   soaking water
1 strip kombu, 2 inches long by 1 inch wide, soaked
4 to 5 shiitake mushrooms, soaked, stems removed, and
   sliced thin
4 to 5 pieces flat fu, soaked and sliced in thin strips or
   cubes
2 to 3 Tbsp shoyu
1/2 cup scallion, sliced thin, for garnish

Place the water, kombu, shiitake, and fu in a pot. Cover
and bring to a boil. Reduce the flame to medium-low and
simmer 10 to 15 minutes. Remove the kombu and set aside
for future use. Add the shoyu, cover, and simmer over a low
flame for 5 minutes. Place in serving bowls and garnish with
chopped fresh scallion.

3
Bean Soups

Bean soups are eaten throughout the world. They are a good source of high-quality vegetable protein. Bean soups are hearty and nourishing and are good complements to whole grains, vegetables, and other natural food dishes. Smaller beans such as azuki, lentil, black soybean, and chickpeas are generally easier to digest and are recommended for regular use. Other beans can be used from time to time. Because of their high content of protein and fat, beans are generally soaked prior to cooking. They also require a slightly longer cooking time than do whole grains and vegetables.

Azuki Pumpkin Soup

4 to 5 cups water, including azuki soaking water
1 cup azuki beans, washed and soaked 6 to 8 hours or
   overnight, reserve soaking water
1 cup Hokkaido pumpkin or buttercup squash, cubed
1 cup onion, diced
1/4 cup celery, diced
1/4 tsp sea salt
several drops of shoyu
2 Tbsp scallion, finely chopped, for garnish

Place the azuki beans and water in a pressure cooker. Cover and bring up to pressure over a high flame. Reduce the flame to medium-low and simmer for 50 minutes. Remove from the flame and let the pressure come down. Remove the cover and add the pumpkin or squash, onion, and celery. Cover and bring to a boil again. Reduce the flame to medium-low, add the sea salt, and cook for another 10 minutes. Add the shoyu and simmer for another 3 to 5 minutes. Place in serving bowls and garnish with chopped scallion.

Quick Azuki Soup with Mochi

4 to 5 cups water
2 cups leftover azuki beans
1/2 cup buttercup or butternut squash, diced
1/4 cup onion, diced
1/4 cup sweet corn, removed from cob
1/4 cup celery, diced
1/2 lb mochi, cubed (about 1 cup)
2 to 3 tsp shoyu
2 Tbsp scallion, finely chopped, for garnish

Place the azuki beans, squash, onion, sweet corn, celery, and water in a pot. Cover and bring to a boil. Reduce the flame to medium-low and simmer for 10 minutes. Add the mochi cubes and shoyu. Cover and simmer another 5 minutes until the mochi is soft. Place in serving bowls and garnish with chopped scallion.

Lentil Vegetable Soup

4 to 5 cups water
1 cup lentils, washed
1/2 cup onion, diced
1/2 cup carrot, diced
1/4 cup celery, diced
1/4 cup burdock, diced

2 cloves garlic, minced (can be omitted)
1 bay leaf (can be omitted)
2 Tbsp parsley, minced
1/4 to 1/2 tsp sea salt

Place the lentils, onion, carrot, celery, burdock, garlic, bay leaf, and water in a pot. Cover and bring to a boil. Reduce the flame to medium-low and simmer for 50 minutes. Add the sea salt and simmer another 10 minutes or so. Add the parsley and simmer 1 to 2 minutes. Place in serving bowls.

Lentil Millet Soup with Smoked Tofu

4 to 5 cups water
1/2 cup lentils, washed
1 cup leftover cooked millet or 1/4 cup uncooked millet, washed
1/2 cup onion, diced
1/4 cup celery, diced
1/2 cup smoked tofu, minced or ground in a hand food mill
1/4 cup carrot, diced
1 clove garlic, minced (can be omitted)
2 tsp corn or sesame oil
1/4 to 1/2 tsp sea salt
2 Tbsp parsley, minced

Heat the oil in a pot. Sauté the garlic and onion for 2 to 3 minutes. Add the lentils, millet, and water. Cover and bring to a boil. Reduce the flame to medium-low and simmer for 45 to 50 minutes Add the onion, celery, and carrot. Cover and simmer 5 minutes. Add the sea salt, cover, and simmer another 10 minutes. Reduce the flame to low and add the smoked tofu and parsley. Simmer 1 to 3 minutes. Place in serving bowls.

Red Lentil and Vegetable Soup

    4 to 5 cups water
    1 cup red lentils, washed
    1/2 cup onion, diced
    1/4 cup celery, diced
    1/4 cup burdock, diced
    1/2 cup green beans, sliced in 1/2 inch lengths
    1/4 cup yellow wax beans, sliced in 1/2 inch lengths
    1/4 to 1/2 tsp sea salt
    1/2 sheet toasted nori, cut in thin strips, for garnish
    2 Tbsp parsley or scallion, finely chopped, for garnish

Place the red lentils and water in a pot, cover, and bring to a boil. Reduce the flame to medium-low and simmer for 45 to 50 minutes. Add the onion, celery, burdock, and green and yellow beans. Cover and simmer 5 minutes. Add the sea salt, cover, and simmer another 10 minutes. Place in serving bowls and garnish with several strips of nori and chopped parsley or scallion.

Split Pea Soup

    4 to 5 cups water
    1 to 1 1/2 cups green split peas, washed
    1/2 cup onion, diced
    1/2 cup carrot, quartered and sliced 1/4 inch thick
    1 Tbsp wakame, washed, soaked, and sliced
    2 Tbsp bonito flakes (can be omitted)
    3 rounds of fu (dried wheat gluten), soaked and sliced
      in bite-sized pieces
    1/8 cup burdock, diced
    1/4 cup celery, diced
    1/4 to 1/2 tsp sea salt
    1/2 cup whole wheat bread cubes
    several drops of shoyu

Place the split peas, onion, carrot, bonito flakes, fu, burdock, celery, and water in a pot. Cover and bring to a boil. Reduce the flame to medium-low and simmer for 50 minutes. Add the wakame and sea salt. Cover and simmer another 15 minutes until soft and creamy. While the soup is cooking, heat a skillet. Place the bread cubes in the skillet and roast evenly, pushing them back and forth with a wooden paddle or spoon. Season with several drops of shoyu. Place the soup in serving bowls and garnish with the roasted croutons.

Navy Bean and Corn Soup

4 to 5 cups water
2 cups sweet corn, removed from cob
1/2 cup navy beans, washed, soaked 6 to 8 hours or
   overnight, discard soaking water
1/2 cup onion, diced
1/4 cup celery, diced
1/4 cup carrot, diced
1/4 tsp sea salt
1 to 2 tsp brown rice vinegar
several drops of shoyu
2 Tbsp scallion, finely chopped, for garnish

Place the beans and water in a pressure cooker. Cover and bring up to pressure over a high flame. Reduce the flame to medium-low. Simmer for 45 to 50 minutes. Remove from the flame and let the pressure come down. Remove the cover. Add the onion, celery, carrot, and sea salt. Cover with a regular lid, not the pressure cooker lid. Bring to a boil and reduce the flame to medium-low. Simmer for 10 to 15 minutes. Add the shoyu and rice vinegar. Simmer another 3 to 5 minutes. Place in serving bowls and garnish with chopped scallion.

Minestrone

1/4 cup kidney beans, washed, soaked 6 to 8 hours or
overnight, discard soaking water
1/4 cup lentils, washed
1/4 cup navy or great northern beans, washed, soaked 6
to 8 hours or overnight, discard soaking water
1 inch kombu, soaked and diced, reserve soaking water
5 cups water
1/4 cup onion, diced
1/4 cup green string beans, stems removed and sliced in
1/2 inch lengths
1/4 cup yellow wax beans, stems removed and sliced in
1/2 inch lengths
1/4 cup celery, diced
1/4 cup carrot, diced
1/8 cup sweet corn, removed from cob
1/8 cup sweet red bell pepper, diced (can be omitted)
1/4 cup leek or escarole, finely chopped
1 cup whole grain elbow or shell pasta, cooked
2 to 2 1/2 Tbsp umeboshi vinegar
1 to 1 1/2 tsp shoyu
2 Tbsp scallion, parsley, or chives, finely chopped, for
garnish

Place the kombu, beans, lentils, and water in a pressure
cooker. Cover and bring up to pressure over a high flame. Reduce the flame to medium-low and simmer for 45 to 50 minutes. Remove from the flame and let the pressure come down.
Remove the cover. Add the onion, green and yellow beans,
carrot, celery, corn, and red pepper. Cover with a regular lid,
not the pressure cooker lid. Bring to a boil. Reduce the flame
to medium-low and simmer another 5 minutes or so. Add the
umeboshi vinegar, shoyu, pasta, leek, and escarole or spinach.
Simmer another 5 minutes. Place in serving bowls and garnish.

Kidney Bean Vegetable Soup

1 1/2 cups kidney beans, washed, soaked 6 to 8 hours or overnight, discard soaking water
4 to 5 cups water
1 cup onion, diced
1/2 cup carrot, diced
1/4 cup celery, diced
1/4 cup sweet corn, removed from cob
1 to 1 1/2 Tbsp miso, puréed
2 Tbsp scallion, finely chopped, for garnish

Place the beans and water in a pressure cooker, cover, and bring up to pressure over a high flame. Reduce the flame to medium-low and simmer for 45 to 50 minutes. Remove from the flame and let the pressure come down. Remove the cover and add the onion, carrot, celery, and sweet corn. Cover with a regular cover, not the pressure cooker lid. Bring to a boil. Reduce the flame to medium-low and simmer another 7 to 10 minutes. Place miso in a cup or bowl, add broth, and dilute with a spoon or chopstick. Turn the flame down to very low and add the puréed miso. Simmer for 2 to 3 minutes. Place in serving bowls and garnish.

Vegetarian Chili

1 cup red chili beans or red kidney beans
4 to 5 cups water
1/4 cup bulghur
1/2 clove garlic, minced (can be omitted)
1/2 cup onion, diced
1/4 cup celery, diced
1/4 cup carrot, diced
1/4 cup green bell pepper, diced (can be omitted)
1/4 cup sweet red pepper, diced (can be omitted)
1/4 cup cooked seitan, finely minced or ground in a

hand food mill
1 tsp umeboshi vinegar
1 1/2 to 2 Tbsp mellow barley miso
1/2 tsp organic red chili powder (can be omitted)
1 to 2 tsp sesame or corn oil

Place the beans and water in a pressure cooker, cover, and bring to pressure. Reduce the flame to medium-low and simmer for 45 to 50 minutes. Remove from the flame and allow the pressure to come down. Remove the cover. Heat the oil in a soup pot. Sauté the garlic and onion for 1 to 3 minutes. Add the carrot, celery, peppers, seitan, bulghur, beans, and cooking liquid. Cover and bring to a boil. Reduce the flame to medium-low and simmer another 20 minutes. Add the umeboshi vinegar, miso, and optional chili powder. Simmer another 3 to 5 minutes. Place in serving bowls.

Pinto Bean Soup

2 cups pinto beans, washed, soaked 6 to 8 hours or overnight, discard soaking water
4 to 5 cups water
1/2 cup onion, diced
1 cup carrot, quartered and sliced in 1/4 to 1/2 inch pieces
1/2 cup sweet corn, removed from cob
1/4 cup yellow summer squash, diced
1/4 cup zucchini, diced (can be omitted)
1/4 to 1/2 tsp sea salt
1/4 cup leek, sliced thin
2 Tbsp scallion, finely chopped, for garnish

Place the beans and water in a pressure cooker, cover, and bring up to pressure. Reduce the flame to medium-low and simmer for 50 to 60 minutes. Remove from the flame and let the pressure come down. Remove the cover. Add the onion, carrot, sweet corn, squash, and zucchini. Cover with a regular lid, not the pressure cooker lid, and bring to a boil.

Reduce the flame to medium-low and simmer 5 minutes. Add the sea salt and leek. Cover and simmer another 10 minutes. Place in serving bowls and garnish.

Lima Bean and Fu Soup

1 cup large lima beans, washed and soaked 6 to 8 hours, discard soaking water
1 inch kombu, soaked and minced
1 cup large rounds of fu, soaked 10 minutes and cubed
1 cup cabbage, sliced into chunks
1/4 cup bonito flakes (can be omitted)
1/4 cup onion, diced
4 to 5 cups water, including fu and kombu soaking water
1/4 to 1/2 tsp sea salt
2 Tbsp scallion, finely sliced, for garnish

Place the lima beans, kombu, fu, and water in a pressure cooker. Cover, place over a high flame, and bring up to pressure. Reduce the flame to medium-low and cook for 40 minutes. Remove from the flame and allow the pressure to come down. Remove the cover and add the cabbage, onion, and sea salt. Place over a high flame and bring to a boil. Cover with a lid (not pressure cooker lid) and reduce the flame to medium-low. Simmer 15 to 20 minutes until the cabbage is tender. Remove and place in serving bowls. Garnish with chopped scallion and serve.

Yellow Soybean and Vegetable Stew

1 cup yellow soybeans, soaked 6 to 8 hours, discard soaking water
1 inch kombu, soaked 3 to 5 minutes and diced
1/4 cup celery, diced
1/4 cup fresh daikon, quartered and sliced 1/4 inch thick

1/2 cup carrot, quartered and sliced 1/4 inch thick
2 ears sweet corn, kernels removed from cob
1/4 cup green string beans, sliced in 1 inch lengths
4 shiitake mushrooms, soaked 10 minutes and diced
1/4 cup fresh or dried lotus root, chopped
1/4 cup fu or seitan, cubed
1/4 cup deep-fried or dried tofu, cubed
5 cups water, including kombu and shiitake soaking
  water
1 1/2 Tbsp shoyu
2 Tbsp scallion, chives, or parsley, finely chopped, for
  garnish

Place the soybeans, kombu, shiitake, and water in a pressure cooker. Cover and bring up to pressure over a high flame. Reduce the flame to medium-low and cook for 45 minutes. Remove from the flame and allow the pressure to come down. Remove the cover. Add the celery, daikon, tofu, fu or seitan, green beans, sweet corn, carrot, and lotus root. Cover with a regular lid and bring to a boil. Reduce the flame to medium-low and simmer for 10 minutes until the vegetables are tender. Season with shoyu and simmer another 4 to 5 minutes. Place in serving bowls and garnish.

Black Bean Soup

1 cup black beans, soaked 6 to 8 hours, discard soaking
  water
4 to 5 cups water
1 cup onion, diced
1/4 cup celery, diced
1/4 cup carrot, diced
1/4 cup sweet corn, removed from cob
1/4 to 1/2 tsp sea salt
2 Tbsp scallion, chives, or parsley, finely chopped, for
  garnish

Place the beans and water in a pot, cover, and bring to a

boil. Reduce the flame to medium-low and simmer 1 1/2 hours until about 80 percent done. Add the onion, celery, carrot, sweet corn, and sea salt. Cover and simmer another 1/2 hour. Place in serving bowls and garnish.

White Bean Soup with Fu

> 1 cup lima, northern, navy, or white kidney beans, soaked 6 to 8 hours
> 5 cups water, including fu soaking water
> 1 cup round fu, soaked and sliced in bite-sized pieces
> 1/4 cup bonito flakes (can be omitted)
> 1/4 cup onion, diced
> 1/2 cup green cabbage, cubed
> 1/4 cup carrot, diced
> 1/4 tsp sea salt
> 1/4 cup parsley or scallion, chopped fine, for garnish

Place the beans, fu, bonito flakes, onion, cabbage, carrot, and water in a pressure cooker. Cover and bring up to pressure. Reduce the flame to medium-low and simmer 45 to 50 minutes. Remove from the flame and allow the pressure to come down. Remove the cover and add the sea salt. Cover with a plain lid, not the pressure cooker top. Place over a medium-low flame and simmer 15 minutes. Place in serving bowls and garnish.

Gazpacho (Chilled Chickpea Soup)

> 2 cup chickpeas, soaked 6 to 8 hours, discard soaking water
> 5 cups water
> 1/8 tsp sea salt
> 1/4 cup carrot, coarsely grated
> 1/4 cup cucumber, sliced in thin matchsticks
> 1 Tbsp scallion or chives, finely minced, for garnish
> 1 tsp minced garlic (can be omitted)

1 cup deep-fried or pan-roasted whole wheat croutons,
   for garnish
1 tsp shoyu

Place the chickpeas and water in a pressure cooker. Cover and bring up to pressure over a high flame. Reduce the flame to medium-low and cook for 1 hour and 15 minutes. Remove from the flame and allow the pressure to come down. Remove the lid and add the sea salt. Place the cooker over a high flame and bring to a boil. Cover with a regular lid, not the pressure cooker lid, and simmer 10 minutes. Remove from the flame and purée in a hand food mill or blender until smooth and creamy. Place in individual bowls. Place the bowls in the refrigerator until slightly chilled.

While the soup is chilling, place the garlic, scallion or chives, carrot, cucumber, and shoyu in a mixing bowl. Mix and allow to marinate while the soup is chilling. When the soup is cool, remove and garnish each bowl with about 1 tablespoon of marinated vegetables and several croutons. Serve cool.

Chickpea and Roasted Red Pepper Soup

1 cup chickpeas, soaked 6 to 8 hours, discard soaking
   water
5 cups water
1 medium red pepper, washed
1/4 cup carrot, diced
1/2 cup onion, diced
1/4 cup zucchini or yellow summer squash, quartered
   and sliced 1/4 inch thick
1/4 cup green string beans, sliced in 1 inch lengths
1/4 cup yellow wax beans, sliced in 1 inch lengths
1 to 2 tsp finely minced garlic (can be omitted)
1 Tbsp extra virgin olive or light sesame oil
1/4 to 1/2 tsp sea salt
2 Tbsp parsley, finely minced, for garnish

Place the water and chickpeas in a pressure cooker, cover, and bring up to pressure. Reduce the flame to medium-low and cook for 1 hour and 15 minutes. Remove from the flame and allow the pressure to come down. Remove the lid, and place over a medium to low flame.

While the chickpeas are cooking, take the red pepper and either place it directly over a burner on the stove on a low flame or in a 400 degree F. oven and roast until the outside skin is charred. Remove and peel the charred skin off the pepper. Remove the seeds. Dice the pepper and then grind with a blender or hand blender.

Place the oil in a skillet and heat. Add the garlic and onion. Sauté 1 to 2 minutes. Place in the pot with the chickpeas. Add the ground red pepper and other vegetables. Cover with a regular lid, not the pressure cooker lid, and bring to a boil. Add the sea salt, cover, and reduce the flame to low. Simmer for 10 minutes. Place in serving bowls and garnish.

Sweet Vegetable Chickpea Soup

> 1 cup chickpeas, soaked 6 to 8 hours, discard soaking water
> 5 cups water
> 1/4 cup onion, diced
> 1/4 cup celery, diced
> 1/4 cup carrot, diced
> 1/4 cup sweet corn, kernels removed from cob
> 1/2 cup buttercup, butternut, or any other sweet hard winter squash, cubed
> 1/4 to 1/2 tsp sea salt
> 2 Tbsp scallion, chives, or parsley, finely chopped, for garnish

Place the chickpeas and water in a pressure cooker, cover, and bring up to pressure. Reduce the flame to medium-low and cook for 1 hour and 15 minutes. Remove from the flame and allow the pressure to come down. Remove the lid and place over a high flame. Add the onion, celery, carrot, sweet corn, and squash. Cover with a regular lid, not the pressure cooker lid, and bring to a boil. Add the sea salt, cover, and reduce the flame to low. Simmer for 10 minutes. Place in serving bowls and garnish.

As a variation, you can season the soup with puréed yellow or white miso instead of sea salt.

Creamy Chickpea Vegetable Soup

> 1 cup chickpeas, soaked 6 to 8 hours, discard soaking
>   water
> 4 to 5 cups water
> 1 inch kombu, soaked and diced
> 1 cup daikon, cubed
> 1 cup carrot, cubed
> 1/4 cup celery, diced
> 1/4 cup leek, sliced in 1/4 inch thick rounds
> 1/4 to 1/2 tsp sea salt
> 2 Tbsp scallion or parsley, finely chopped, for garnish

Place the chickpeas, water, and kombu in a pressure cooker. Cover and bring up to pressure. Reduce the flame to medium-low and cook for 1 hour and 15 minutes. Remove from the flame and allow the pressure to come down. Remove the lid. Add the daikon, carrot, and celery. Cover with a regular lid, not the pressure cooker lid, and bring to a boil. Add the sea salt, cover, and reduce the flame to low. Simmer for 10 minutes. Add the leek, cover, and simmer 2 to 3 minutes. Place in serving bowls and garnish.

4
Vegetable Soups

Vegetables reflect nature's seasonal abundance. They comprise the main side dishes in a broad-based macrobiotic diet. They complement whole grains and beans and can be used in soups and other dishes in which these foods are the main ingredients. Miso soups are based on the use of vegetables from both land and sea. The vegetable soups in this chapter highlight the use of land vegetables and seasonings such as shoyu and sea salt. They come in three main varieties: clear broth soups, creamy vegetable soups, and vegetable purées. Vegetable soups can be served hot when the weather is cold and chilled when the weather is hot. As much as possible, try to use vegetables that are organically grown. When organic produce is not available, you can use supermarket produce. The essential point is to have plenty of variety. The most healthful soups are those in which you rely on vegetables produced in your climatic zone. Thus, if you live in the temperate zone, try not to rely on tropical vegetables or nightshades such as tomato, potato, eggplant, or hot peppers, all of which originated in tropical or equatorial regions.

French Onion Soup

2 to 2 1/2 cups onions, sliced in thin half-moons
4 to 5 cups water, including kombu and shiitake soak-
    ing water
1 inch kombu, soaked and diced
4 shiitake mushrooms, soaked, stems removed, and
    diced
1 Tbsp bonito flakes (can be omitted)
2 tsp dark sesame oil
1 cup plain mochi, cubed
2 to 3 Tbsp shoyu
1/2 cup deep-fried or pan-roasted croutons, for garnish
2 Tbsp scallion or parsley, finely chopped, for garnish

Heat the oil in a pot. Add the onions and sauté for 4 to 5
minutes until translucent. Add the kombu, shiitake, bonito
flakes, and water. Cover and bring to a boil. Reduce the flame
to medium-low and simmer for 25 to 30 minutes. Add the
shoyu, cover, and simmer for another 5 minutes. While the
soup is simmering, heat a skillet and brown the mochi until
each piece puffs up. When the soup is done, place in serving
bowls. Garnish each with several pieces of mochi and croutons. Garnish with chopped scallion or parsley.

Puréed Cauliflower Soup

1 medium head cauliflower, chopped
4 to 5 cups water
1/4 to 1/2 tsp sea salt
4 to 5 lemon slices, cut in half-moons, for garnish
2 Tbsp parsley, finely minced, for garnish

Place the cauliflower and water in a pot. Cover and bring
to a boil. Reduce the flame to medium-low and simmer for 10
minutes. Add the sea salt and cook another 5 minutes until
soft. Purée the cauliflower and liquid through a hand food

mill. Place back in the pot. Simmer another 5 minutes. Place in serving bowls and garnish each with a half-moon slice of lemon and parsley.

Puréed Squash Soup

1 medium-sized buttercup squash or Hokkaido pumpkin, skin removed and cubed
4 to 5 cups water
1/4 to 1/2 tsp sea salt
1/2 cup onion, minced
2 Tbsp scallion, chives, or parsley, finely chopped, for garnish

Place the water and squash in a pot, cover, and bring to a boil. Reduce the flame to medium-low and simmer 10 minutes until soft. Remove and purée the squash and cooking water through a hand food mill. Place back on the stove, and add the sea salt and onion. Cover and bring to a boil. Reduce the flame to medium-low and simmer 10 minutes. Place in serving bowls and garnish. As a variation, try seasoning the soup with a little puréed miso instead of sea salt.

Puréed Summer Squash Soup

4 to 5 cups water
4 cups summer squash, diced
1/4 to 1/2 tsp sea salt
2 Tbsp parsley, minced, for garnish

Place the squash, sea salt, and water in a pot. Cover and bring to a boil. Reduce the flame to medium-low and simmer 10 minutes. Puree' the squash and liquid through a hand food mill. Place in a pot over a low flame. Simmer 2 to 3 minutes. Place in serving bowls and garnish.

Puréed Carrot Soup

3 cups carrot, finely grated
4 to 5 cups water
1 cup onion, finely minced
1/4 tsp sea salt
1/2 sheet nori, toasted and cut in thin strips, for garnish
2 Tbsp scallion, chives, or parsley, finely chopped, for
  garnish

Place the carrot, water, onion, and sea salt in a pot. Cover and bring to a boil. Reduce the flame to medium-low and simmer for 20 to 25 minutes. Place in serving bowls and garnish with several strips of nori and chopped scallion, chives, or parsley.

Puréed Broccoli Soup with Tofu Sour Cream

1 medium-sized head of broccoli, finely chopped
4 to 5 cups water
1/4 tsp sea salt
1/2 lb firm style tofu
1/4 cup water
1/4 tsp shoyu
1 1/2 Tbsp umeboshi vinegar
1 Tbsp onion, finely grated
1 Tbsp carrot, finely grated, for garnish
1/2 sheet nori, toasted and cut in thin strips, for garnish

Place the broccoli, water, and sea salt in a pot. Cover and bring to a boil. Reduce the flame to medium-low and simmer for 20 minutes until soft. Pureé the broccoli and cooking liquid through a hand food mill. Place in a pot and cook over a low flame for 2 to 3 minutes. While the broccoli is cooking, place the tofu, shoyu, umeboshi vinegar, water, and onion in a blender. Puree' until smooth and creamy. Remove and place in a serving bowl. When the soup is done, place in serving bowls and garnish each with 1 to 2 tablespoonfuls of tofu sour cream, a few strips of nori, and a dab of grated carrot.

Borscht

2 cups red cabbage, finely shredded
1 cup beet, peeled and finely minced
1 cup onion, minced
4 to 5 cups water
1 Tbsp bonito flakes (can be omitted)
1 to 1 1/2 tsp corn oil
1/4 tsp sea salt
1/2 lb firm style tofu
1/4 cup water
1/2 tsp shoyu
1 1/2 to 2 tsp umeboshi vinegar
1 Tbsp onion, finely grated
2 tsp brown rice vinegar
1 cup whole wheat croutons, pan-fried or toasted

Place the oil in a pot and heat. Add the onion and sautéed for 1 to 2 minutes. Add the beet, bonito flakes, and half the water measurement. Cover and bring to a boil. Reduce the flame to medium-low and simmer 20 minutes. Add the cabbage, sea salt, and brown rice vinegar. Cover and simmer another 10 to 15 minutes until the vegetables are very tender. While the soup is cooking, place the tofu, water, shoyu, umeboshi vinegar, and onion in a blender. Puree' until smooth and creamy. Place in a serving bowl. When the soup is done, place in serving bowls. Garnish bowl with 1 to 2 tablespoonfuls of puréed tofu sour cream and several croutons.

Cabbage Soup

1 cup onion, minced
2 cups green cabbage, finely shredded
1/2 cup carrot, coarsely grated

2 tsp dark sesame oil
4 to 5 cups water
1/4 to 1/2 tsp sea salt
1/2 cup tofu sour cream (see previous recipes)
2 Tbsp parsley, finely minced
1/4 tsp caraway seeds (can be omitted)

Heat the oil in a pot. Sauté the onion for 3 to 4 minutes. Add the cabbage, carrot, and water. Cover and bring to a boil. Reduce the flame to medium-low and simmer 20 minutes. Add the sea salt and caraway seeds. Simmer another 10 to 15 minutes. Place in serving bowls and garnish each with 1 to 2 tablespoonfuls of tofu sour cream and a little parsley.

Grated Daikon Soup

2 cups finely grated daikon
4 to 5 cups water, including kombu and shiitake soak-
    ing water
1 inch kombu, soaked
4 to 5 shiitake mushrooms, soaked, stems removed, and
    diced
1/4 to 1/2 tsp sea salt
1/4 cup scallion, finely sliced

Place the water, kombu, and shiitake in a pot. Cover and bring to a boil. Reduce the flame to medium and simmer for 5 minutes. Remove the kombu and set aside. You may use it later in other dishes. Cover and simmer the shiitake for another 5 minutes. Add the daikon and sea salt. Cover and simmer over a medium-low flame for another 10 minutes. Place in serving bowls and garnish with chopped scallion.

As a variation, you may add a tablespoonful of natto (whole fermented soybeans) to each bowl of soup as you serve. Cubed tofu can also be added to the soup toward the end of cooking. Simmer the tofu for 2 to 3 minutes before serving.

Cream of Corn Soup

3 cups sweet corn, removed from cob with a box grater
1 cup leftover soft brown rice porridge, puréed in a
hand food mill
1/2 cup onion, minced
1/4 cup celery, minced
1 tsp corn oil (can be omitted)
4 to 5 cups water
1/4 to 1/2 tsp sea salt
2 Tbsp parsley, minced, for garnish
1/2 tsp organic cayenne pepper, for garnish (can be
omitted)

Heat the oil in a pot and sauté the onions for 2 to 3 minutes. Add the celery, corn, rice, and water. Cover and bring to a boil. Reduce the flame to medium-low and simmer for 10 to 15 minutes. Add the sea salt, cover, and simmer another 10 minutes. Place in serving bowls and garnish with parsley and a dash of cayenne pepper.

Leek and Mushroom Soup

4 to 5 cups water
2 cups leeks, sliced thin
1 cup mushrooms, sliced thin
2 Tbsp shoyu
2 Tbsp parsley, minced, for garnish
1 tsp sesame oil (can be omitted)

Heat the oil in a pot and sauté the mushrooms for 3 to 5 minutes. Add the water, cover, and bring to a boil. Reduce the flame to medium-low and simmer 5 minutes. Add the leeks, cover, and simmer 3 minutes. Add the shoyu, cover, and simmer another 3 to 5 minutes. Place in serving bowls and garnish with chopped parsley. For a refreshingly cool summer soup, blend the soup when done and chill slightly.

Vichyssoise (Leek and Taro, or Leek and Jinenjo Soup)

    2 large leeks (2 to 3 cups), minced
    1/2 cup onion, minced
    2 to 3 cups taro potato or jinenjo, peeled and sliced thin
      (if using jinenjo, do not peel)
    1 Tbsp corn oil
    1/3 cup unbleached white flour
    5 cups water
    1/4 to 1/2 tsp sea salt
    1 cup tofu cream (see previous recipes, omit rice vine-
      gar)
    1/8 cup chives, scallion, or watercress, finely chopped,
      for garnish

    Heat the oil in a pot. Add the onion and leeks. Sauté 2 to
3 minutes. Slowly mix in the flour and sauté another 1 to 2
minutes until the flour completely coats the vegetables. Add
the taro potatoes and mix. Gradually add the water, stirring
constantly to prevent lumping, until smooth. Cover and bring
to a boil. Reduce the flame to medium-low and simmer for 10
minutes. Add the sea salt, cover, and simmer another 10 minutes. Remove and purée through a hand food mill or blender.
Place back in a pot and heat. Stir in the tofu cream and place
in serving bowls. Garnish and serve.

Cream of Celery Soup

    2 cups celery, diced
    1/2 cup onion, minced
    1 to 1 1/2 cups leftover cooked brown rice
    4 to 5 cups water
    2 tsp corn oil
    1/4 to 1/2 tsp sea salt
    2 Tbsp chives, scallion, or parsley, minced, for garnish

Place the water and rice in a pot, cover, and bring to a boil. Reduce the flame to medium-low and simmer 15 to 20 minutes until the rice is soft and creamy. Remove and purée in a hand food mill. While the rice is cooking, heat the oil in a skillet and sauté the onion for 2 to 3 minutes. Add the celery and sauté another 3 to 4 minutes. Place the puréed rice and sautéed vegetables in a pot. Cover and bring to a boil. Reduce the flame to medium-low and simmer for 15 minutes. Add the sea salt and simmer another 10 minutes. Place in serving bowls and garnish.

Cream of Mushroom Soup

    2 cups mushrooms, diced
    1 cup onion, diced
    1/4 cup celery, diced
    1 Tbsp corn oil
    1/3 to 1/2 cup unbleached white flour
    2 to 2 1/2 Tbsp shoyu
    2 Tbsp parsley, minced, for garnish

Heat the oil in a pot, add the onion, and sauté 2 to 3 minutes. Add the mushrooms and a few drops of shoyu. Sauté 4 to 5 minutes. Slowly add the flour to the vegetables, stirring constantly. Sauté 1 to 2 minutes. Slowly add the water, stirring constantly to prevent lumping. Stir constantly until the liquid comes to a boil. If lumps do form, use a wire whisk to dissolve them. Cover and bring to a boil. Reduce the flame to medium-low and simmer about 15 minutes. Add the shoyu and simmer another 5 to 7 minutes. Place in serving bowls and garnish.

Cream of Vegetable Soup

    4 to 5 cups water
    1 cup leftover cooked brown rice
    1/2 cup oatmeal flakes

1 Tbsp corn oil
1/2 cup onion, minced
1/2 cup carrot, diced
1/4 cup celery, diced
1/4 cup green peas, shelled
1/2 cup cauliflower, cut into small flowerets
1/4 cup rutabaga, diced
1/4 to 1/2 tsp sea salt
2 Tbsp parsley, chives, or scallion, minced, for garnish

Place the rice, oats, and water in a pot. Cover and bring to a boil. Reduce the flame to medium-low and simmer for 15 to 20 minutes until creamy. Remove and purée in a hand food mill. Place back in a pot, cover, and bring to a boil. While the rice and oats are cooking, heat the oil in a skillet and sauté the onion for 3 to 5 minutes. When the rice has been puréed and placed back in the pot, add the sautéed onion, along with with celery, carrot, peas, cauliflower, and rutabaga. Cover and bring to a boil. Reduce the flame to medium-low and simmer for 5 minutes. Add the sea salt, cover, and simmer another 10 to 15 minutes until the vegetables are tender. Place in serving bowls and garnish.

Creamy Turnip or Rutabaga Soup

3 cups turnip or rutabaga, diced
1 cup onion, diced
1/2 cup celery and celery leaves, finely chopped
5 cups water
1/2 cup oatmeal flakes
1/4 to 1/2 tsp sea salt
2 Tbsp fresh lemon juice
2 Tbsp chives or parsley, finely chopped, for garnish
1 Tbsp dulse (sea vegetable), soaked and diced, for garnish
1 tsp corn oil

Heat the oil in a pot. Sauté the onion and celery for 2 to 3 minutes. Add the turnip or rutabaga, water, and oatmeal. Cover and bring to a boil. Reduce the flame to medium-low and simmer 5 minutes. Add the sea salt, cover, and simmer another 15 minutes. Remove from the stove and purée all liquid and vegetables through a hand food mill. Place back in the pot and heat. Add the lemon juice and simmer 1 to 2 minutes. Place in serving bowls and garnish each bowl with a little dulse and chives or parsley.

Ume Vegetable Soup

1/4 cup onion, diced
1/4 cup celery, diced
1/2 cup carrot, diced
1/2 cup sweet corn, removed from cob
1/4 cup green peas, shelled
1/4 cup green string beans, sliced in 1 inch lengths
1/4 cup yellow wax beans, sliced in 1 inch lengths
1/4 cup fresh lima beans
5 cups water
2 to 3 Tbsp umeboshi vinegar
2 Tbsp chives or parsley, minced, for garnish

Place the onion, celery, carrot, corn, peas, green beans, wax beans, and lima beans in a pot. Add the water, cover, and bring to a boil. Reduce the flame to medium-low and simmer 5 to 7 minutes. Add the umeboshi vinegar, cover, and simmer over a low flame for another 4 to 5 minutes. Place in serving bowls and garnish. As a variation, try adding 1/2 cup cooked elbow or shell noodles or cooked barley to the above recipe. Let these ingredients simmer for 2 to 3 minutes.

Kenchin (Kuzu Vegetable) Soup

4 to 5 cups water, including shiitake soaking water
1/2 cup onion, diced
1/4 cup celery, diced

1/4 cup carrot, diced
1/8 cup burdock, diced
1/4 cup daikon, diced
1/2 cup Chinese cabbage, finely chopped
4 shiitake mushrooms, soaked, stems removed, and
   diced
1/2 cup tofu, cubed and deep-fried until golden
3 1/2 to 4 Tbsp kuzu, diluted
2 Tbsp shoyu
1 tsp sesame oil
2 Tbsp scallion, finely chopped, for garnish

Heat the oil in a pot. Sauté the onion for 1 to 2 minutes. Add the celery, carrot, burdock, daikon, shiitake, and deep-fried tofu cubes. Add the water, cover, and bring to a boil. Reduce the flame to medium-low and simmer for 5 to 7 minutes. Add the Chinese cabbage. Add the diluted kuzu, stirring constantly to prevent lumping. Add the shoyu and simmer for another 3 to 5 minutes. Place in serving bowls and garnish.

Sweet Pumpkin Soup

4 cups sugar baby pumpkin (used for pumpkin pie),
   cubed
4 to 5 cups water
1/4 to 1/2 tsp sea salt
1/8 tsp cinnamon (can be omitted)
1/8 tsp nutmeg (can be omitted)
1/4 cup brown rice syrup
1 Tbsp parsley, minced, for garnish

Place the pumpkin and water in a pot. Cover and bring to a boil. Reduce the flame to medium-low and simmer 10 minutes until the pumpkin is soft. Purée through a hand food mill and place back in the pot over a medium-low flame. Add the sea salt, cinnamon, and nutmeg. Cover and simmer for another 10 minutes. Add the rice syrup and simmer 2 to 3 minutes. Place in serving bowls and garnish.

Sake Lees Soup

Sake lees is the byproduct left from brewing sake, or rice wine. It is the sediment or residue that remains after the process of fermentation is complete. Sake lees is white or off-white in color and has a texture similar to certain varieties of cheese. You can find sake lees in the refrigerator section of Japanese food markets. Soup made with sake lees has a warming effect and is especially nice in cold weather.

    4 to 5 cups water
    1/3 cup sake lees
    1 cup daikon, cut in matchsticks
    1 cup carrot, cut in matchsticks
    3 to 4 slices firm style tofu, deep-fried until golden and
      cut into thin strips
    1/2 cup onion, diced
    pinch sea salt
    2 Tbsp shoyu
    1/4 cup scallion, sliced thin, for garnish

Place the onion, daikon, carrot, tofu, and water in a pot. Add a pinch of sea salt, cover, and bring to a boil. Reduce the flame to medium-low and simmer 7 to 10 minutes until the vegetables are tender. Break the sake lees into small pieces and place in a suribachi. Add a little water and purée to a smooth paste as you would if puréeing miso. Add the sake lees and shoyu to the soup, cover, and simmer for another 10 minutes over a low flame. Place in serving bowls and garnish. This soup is especially delicious when you add bonito (dried fish) flakes or finely chopped crabmeat at the end of cooking.

Jinenjo Soup

Jinenjo is a variety of mountain potato grown in Japan. It is not related to the regular potato and can be eaten for its strengthening effects. It can be found in Japanese food stores.

    4 to 5 cups water, including shiitake and kombu soak-

ing water
1 to 1 1/2 cups jinenjo, finely grated
4 to 5 shiitake mushrooms, soaked, stems removed, and
sliced thin
4 to 5 sprigs watercress, boiled for 1 minute and
drained
3 slices lemon, cut in half-moons
2 Tbsp shoyu
1 inch kombu, soaked

Place the shiitake, kombu, and water in a pot. Cover and bring to a boil. Reduce the flame to medium-low and simmer 5 minutes. Remove the kombu and set aside. You may use it later in other dishes. Cover and simmer the shiitake another 5 minutes. Add the grated jinenjo and shoyu. Stir and simmer over a low flame for another 5 minutes. Place in serving bowls and garnish each with a sprig of watercress and half a slice of lemon.

Watercress and Carrot Flower Soup

4 to 5 cups water, including kombu and shiitake soaking water
4 to 5 shiitake mushrooms, soaked, stems removed, and
quartered
1 strip kombu, 2 inches by 1 inch, soaked
1/2 bunch watercress
1/2 cup carrot, cut in flower shapes
2 to 3 Tbsp shoyu

Place the water, shiitake, and kombu in a pot. Cover and bring to a boil. Reduce the flame to medium-low and simmer 5 minutes. Remove the kombu and set aside for later use. Cover and simmer another 5 minutes. Add the carrot, cover, and simmer 1 to 2 minutes. Reduce the flame to low, add the shoyu, and simmer 3 to 5 minutes. Place a little watercress in each serving bowl. Ladle the hot broth and carrot flowers over the watercress and serve.

Clear Broth Soup

1/2 cup taro potato, peeled and cubed
4 to 5 cups water, including shiitake and kombu soak-
    ing water
2 cups Chinese cabbage, sliced
4 to 5 shiitake mushrooms, soaked, stems removed, and
    quartered
1 inch kombu, soaked
1/2 cup carrot, cut in matchsticks
2 to 3 Tbsp shoyu
1 tsp ginger juice
2 Tbsp scallion, finely sliced, for garnish

Place the kombu, shiitake, and water in a pot. Cover and
bring to a boil. Reduce the flame to medium-low and simmer
5 minutes. Remove the kombu and set aside for later use.
Add the taro, cover, and simmer another 5 minutes. Add the
shoyu, cover, and simmer 5 minutes. Add the Chinese cabbage and ginger juice. Simmer 1 minute. Place in serving
bowls and garnish.

Cool Cucumber Soup

5 cups cucumber, peeled, seeds removed, and sliced
4 to 5 cups water
1/4 to 1/2 tsp sea salt
3 slices lemon, cut in half-moons, for garnish
1 Tbsp fresh dill or chives, minced

Place the cucumber, water, and sea salt in a pot. Cover
and bring to a boil. Reduce the flame to medium-low and
simmer 10 minutes. Purée in a blender. Place in the refrigerator and chill. Remove, place in serving bowls, and garnish
with a slice of lemon and a little dill or chives.

Escarole Soup

    4 to 5 cups water
    1 Tbsp extra virgin olive oil
    2 cloves garlic, minced
    4 cups escarole, chopped
    1 cup onion, minced
    1/4 to 1/2 tsp sea salt
    1/2 cup mushrooms, diced
    3 slices lemon, cut in half-moons, for garnish

Heat the oil in a pot. Sauté the garlic and onion for 2 to 3 minutes. Add the mushrooms and sauté 1 to 2 minutes. Add the water and escarole. Cover and bring to a boil. Reduce the flame to medium-low. Add the sea salt and escarole. Cover and simmer 10 minutes. Puree all ingredients through a hand food mill and place back in the pot over a low flame. Heat and place in serving bowls. Garnish each bowl with a slice of lemon.

Seitan Vegetable Stew

    4 to 5 cups water
    2 cups cooked seitan, cubed
    1/4 cup mushrooms, sliced
    1/4 cup onion, diced
    1/4 cup carrot, diced
    1/4 cup celery, diced
    1/4 cup sweet corn, removed from cob
    1/4 cup turnip or rutabaga, cubed
    2 to 3 Tbsp shoyu
    3 to 4 Tbsp kuzu, diluted
    4 to 5 Tbsp water, for diluting kuzu
    1/4 cup scallion, sliced thin, for garnish

Place the seitan, mushrooms, onion, carrot, celery, corn, turnip or rutabaga, and water in a pot. Cover and bring to a boil. Simmer 10 minutes until all vegetables are tender. Add the kuzu, stirring constantly until thick. Add the shoyu, cover, and simmer another 4 to 5 minutes. Place in serving bowls and garnish.

Fu and Green Pea Soup

> 4 to 5 cups water, including shiitake, fu, and kombu soaking water
> 4 to 5 shiitake mushrooms, soaked, stems removed, and diced
> 1 strip kombu, 2 inches long, soaked
> 8 rounds fu, soaked and sliced in bite-sized pieces
> 2 cups green peas, removed from shell
> 1/4 cup onion, diced
> 1/8 cup carrot, diced
> 2 to 3 Tbsp shoyu
> 1/4 cup scallion or chives, sliced thin, for garnish

Place the kombu, shiitake, fu, and water in a pot. Cover and bring to a boil. Reduce the flame to medium-low and simmer 4 to 5 minutes. Remove the kombu and set aside for future use. Add the green peas, onion, and carrot. Cover and simmer another 5 minutes. Season with shoyu and simmer another 5 minutes. Place in serving bowls and garnish.

5
Noodle and Pasta Soups

In Japan, noodles are a staple in the diet. The most commonly used varieties are soba (buckwheat and wheat noodles), udon (wheat noodles), and somen (thin wheat noodles). Noodles are often served in a delicious broth made from shoyu and kombu. The preparation of this soup broth, called *dashi*, is considered an art.

Noodles in broth are a meal in themselves. My husband, who is a noodle connoisseur, loves to recount the story of the memorable bowl of noodles he enjoyed recently at a traditional soba restaurant in Tokyo. It was a chilly December evening and he had spent the entire day on the train. He was cold and hungry. On the way to the restaurant with his Japanese host, he kept eyeing the take-out sushi offered by sidewalk vendors, thinking that a bowl of noodles wouldn't be enough to satisfy his hunger. At the restaurant he ordered soba in broth topped with tempura. The noodles were served in a hand-made ceramic bowl with a small side dish of finely cut scallion for garnish. The noodles were cooked al dente and blended perfectly with the piping hot broth, which was flavored with just the right degree of saltiness. After savoring this simple delicacy, my husband felt energized and renewed. The hot soup banished the December chill and was so hearty and satisfying that he forgot all about stopping for sushi afterwards.

One of the keys to making delicious and healthful noodles in broth is to select the highest quality natural ingredients. The quality of the soy sauce you use in preparing the broth is especially vital. Like miso, the best shoyu is made from organic soybeans that have been naturally fermented for at least eighteen months. High-quality natural shoyu is available in natural food stores. The shoyu sold commercially in most Oriental markets is not made from organic ingredients. It is often fermented artificially and may contain sugar or synthetic additives.

Another key to making noodles in broth is to use garnishes to achieve balance. Finely chopped scallion (green onion) is the most commonly used garnish for noodle soups. Scallions have a light upward energy that balances the contractive energy of the salty broth and noodles, especially when buckwheat noodles (soba) are used. Other garnishes such as toasted nori and finely grated daikon and carrot also help create balance. In addition to Japanese-style noodles in broth, in this chapter I also present several healthful recipes that utilize whole Italian pastas.

Udon in Broth

2 packages udon (16 oz)
4 to 5 cups water
1 strip kombu, 2 to 3 inches long, soaked
2 to 3 Tbsp shoyu
1/4 cup scallion, thinly sliced, for garnish
2 to 3 qts water, for cooking udon

Place 2 to 3 quarts water in a pot, cover, and bring to a boil. Add the udon and cook as you would spaghetti. When done, place in a strainer and rinse under cold water. Place the kombu and water in a pot. Cover and bring to a boil. Reduce the flame to medium-low and simmer 10 minutes. Add the shoyu and simmer another 5 minutes. Place the udon in serving bowls and pour the hot shoyu broth over them. Garnish with freshly cut scallion.

Somen in Broth

4 to 5 cups water, including kombu and shiitake soaking water
4 to 5 shiitake mushrooms, soaked, stems removed, and sliced thin
1 strip kombu, 2 to 3 inches long, soaked
16 oz somen, cooked, rinsed, and drained
2 to 3 Tbsp shoyu
1 cup tofu, cubed
1 sheet nori, toasted and cut into thin strips, for garnish
1/4 cup scallion, finely chopped, for garnish
4 to 5 Tbsp daikon, finely grated, for garnish
2 Tbsp carrot, finely grated, for garnish

Place the water, kombu, and shiitake in a pot. Cover and bring to a boil. Reduce the flame to medium-low and simmer 5 minutes. Remove the kombu and set aside for later use. Cover and simmer another 5 minutes. Reduce the flame to low and add the shoyu. Cover and simmer another 5 minutes. Add the tofu and simmer for 2 minutes. Cook the somen as you would spaghetti. Place the cooked somen in serving bowls and pour the hot broth over them. Garnish each bowl with 1 tablespoon grated daikon, 1 teaspoon grated carrot, several strips of nori, and freshly cut scallion.

Soba in Broth

2 packages soba (16 oz), cooked
1 strip kombu, 4 inches long, soaked, reserve soaking water
4 to 5 cups water, including kombu soaking water
2 to 3 Tbsp shoyu
1 sheet nori, toasted, cut in 1 inch squares or thin strips, for garnish
4 to 5 Tbsp daikon, finely grated, for garnish
1/4 cup scallion, finely sliced, for garnish

Place the kombu and water in a pot. Cover, bring to a boil, and reduce the flame to medium-low. Simmer for 5 minutes. Add shoyu and simmer another 5 to 7 minutes. Place the cooked soba in serving bowls and ladle hot broth over each serving. Place 1 tablespoonful of grated daikon on top of each bowl of soba. Garnish with several squares or strips of nori and 2 to 3 teaspoonfuls of chopped scallion.

Winter Udon

This dish has a nice warming effect and is epecially good during cold weather.

2 packages udon (16 oz), cooked
4 to 5 shiitake mushrooms, soaked, stems removed, and thinly sliced
1 strip kombu, 4 inches long, soaked
4 to 5 deep-fried tofu strips, 2 inches wide by 3 inches long by 1/2-inch thick (deep-fry until golden and then slice into thin strips)
light sesame oil, for deep-frying tofu
4 to 5 Tbsp kuzu, diluted
5 to 6 cups water, including shiitake and kombu soaking water
1 cup onion, finely diced or minced
2 to 3 Tbsp shoyu
1/4 cup bonito flakes, for garnish (can be omitted)
1 Tbsp fresh ginger, grated, for garnish
1 sheet nori, toasted and cut in thin strips, for garnish
1/4 cup scallion, finely sliced, for garnish

Place the shiitake, kombu, and water in a pot. Cover and bring to a boil. Reduce the flame to medium-low and simmer for 5 minutes. Remove the kombu and set aside to use in other dishes. Cover and simmer another 5 minutes. Add the deep-fried tofu strips and onion. Cover and simmer another 5 minutes. Add the diluted kuzu, stirring constanly to prevent lumping. When the liquid has thickened, add the shoyu and reduce the flame to low. Cover and simmer another 5 minutes. Place the cooked udon in the thickened broth and simmer for 1 to 2 minutes, just enough to heat the udon.

Place the udon, thickened broth, and tofu in serving bowls. Garnish each with 2 to 3 teaspoons of bonito flakes, several strips of nori, 1/4 teaspoon grated ginger, and 2 to 3 teaspoons of chopped scallion. Serve piping hot. For those who wish to avoid oil, do not deep-fry the tofu. Simply cube the tofu and add it to the broth at the same time as the shoyu.

Udon with Fried Tempeh

2 packages udon (16 oz), cooked
4 to 5 cups water, including shiitake and kombu soaking water
4 to 5 shiitake, soaked, stems removed, and sliced or diced
1 strip kombu, 4 inches long, soaked
2 to 3 Tbsp shoyu
1 lb tempeh, any kind, cubed or sliced in strips and deep-fried untilgolden
light sesame oil, for deep-frying tempeh
5 to 10 sprigs watercress, for garnish
4 to 5 Tbsp daikon, finely grated, for garnish
1/4 cup scallion or chives, sliced thin, for garnish
1/4 cup carrot, sliced in matchsticks or flower shapes and par-boiled, for garnish

Place the shiitake, kombu, and water in a pot. Cover and bring to a boil. Reduce the flame to medium-low and simmer for 5 minutes. Remove the kombu and set aside for future use. Cover and simmer another 5 minutes. Add the shoyu and deep-fried tempeh, cover, and simmer another 5 minutes. Place the cooked noodles in serving bowls. Place 2 sprigs of watercress on top of each serving. Ladle the hot broth over the noodles, tempeh, and watercress. Garnish each bowl with 1 tablespoonful of grated daikon, several pieces of carrot matchsticks or flowers, and 2 to 3 tablespoonfuls of sliced scallion or chives.

Tempura Noodles

2 packages udon, somen, or soba (16 oz), cooked
4 to 5 cups water, including kombu soaking water
1 strip kombu, 4 inches long, soaked
2 to 3 Tbsp shoyu
4 to 5 slices buttercup, butternut, or yellow summer
    squash
4 to 5 mushrooms, stems trimmed
4 to 5 broccoli spears or flowerets
4 to 5 summer squash slices
1/4 cup scallion, sliced thin, for garnish
1 tsp ginger, freshly grated, for garnish
light sesame oil, for deep-frying

Tempura Batter
1 cup whole wheat pastry flour
1/2 cup corn flour
1/2 cup brown rice or unbleached white flour
2 Tbsp kuzu, diluted
1/4 tsp sea salt
2 to 2 1/2 cups sparkling or spring water

Place the water and kombu in a pot. Cover and bring to a boil. Reduce the flame to medium-low and simmer 10 minutes. Add the shoyu, cover, and simmer for 5 minutes. Reduce the flame to very low and keep warm until the tempura is ready.

Place 2 to 3 inches of oil in a deep-frying pot and heat. While the oil is heating, place the flour and salt in a mixing bowl. Mix thoroughly. Gradually add the water and diluted kuzu. Place the batter in the freezer for 15 to 20 minutes. Place 4 to 5 vegetable slices in the batter, completely coating them. When the oil is hot place the batter-dipped vegetables in the hot oil. Deep-fry until golden brown. Remove and drain on paper towels. Pre-heat the oven to 180 degrees F. and place the first batch of deep-fried vegetables in it to keep warm while you are frying your next batch. Continue deep-frying 4 to 5 pieces at a time until all the vegetables have been cooked.

Place the cooked noodles in serving bowls and ladle the hot broth over them. Place 1 piece of each kind of tempura on top of the noodles and broth. Garnish with 1/4 teaspoon fresh ginger and 1 tablespoon scallion. Serve hot.

Udon in Thick Broth

> 2 packages udon (16 oz), cooked
> 4 to 5 cups water, including shiitake and kombu soaking water
> 4 to 5 shiitake mushrooms, soaked, stems removed, and quartered
> 1 strip kombu, 2 inches long , soaked
> 2 to 3 Tbsp shoyu
> 1/4 cup onion, diced
> 1/4 cup carrot, diced
> 1/4 cup cooked seitan (can be omitted)
> 1/4 cup snowpeas
> 1/4 cup green string beans, sliced in 1 inch long pieces
> 3 Tbsp kuzu, diluted
> 4 Tbsp water, for diluting kuzu
> 1 sheet nori, toasted and sliced in thin strips or squares, for garnish
> 2 Tbsp tan sesame seeds, roasted, for garnish
> 1/4 cup scallion, sliced thin, for garnish

Place the water, shiitake, and kombu in a pot. Cover and bring to a boil. Reduce the flame to medium-low and simmer 5 minutes. Remove the kombu and set aside for future use. Place the onion, carrot, seitan, and string beans in the pot. Cover and simmer 2 to 3 minutes. Add the diluted kuzu, stirring constantly until the broth is thickened. Reduce the flame to very low and add the shoyu. Cover and simmer another 3 minutes. Add the snowpeas and simmer another minute until they are bright green in color. Do not overcook them. Place the cooked udon in serving bowls and ladle the thick hot broth and vegetables over each serving. Garnish with several strips of nori, a teaspoon of roasted sesame seeds and about 1 tablespoon sliced scallion.

Alphabet Pasta Soup

> 2 cups whole wheat alphabet pasta, cooked
> 4 to 5 cups water, including kombu soaking water
> 1 strip kombu, 2 inches long, soaked
> 4 to 5 fresh shiitake, diced
> 1/4 cup onion, diced
> 1/4 cup carrot, diced
> 1/4 cup green peas, shelled
> 1/4 cup yellow wax beans, cut in 1 inch lengths
> 1/2 cup tofu, cubed
> 2 to 3 Tbsp shoyu or umeboshi vinegar
> 1 sheet nori, toasted and cut in thin strips, for garnish
> 1/4 cup parsley, minced, for garnish

Place the water and kombu in a pot. Cover and bring to a boil. Reduce the flame to medium and simmer 5 minutes. Remove the kombu and set aside for future use. Add the shiitake, onion, carrot, green peas, and wax beans. Cover and simmer for 1 to 2 minutes. Add the cooked pasta and season either with shoyu or umeboshi vinegar. Cover and simmer over a low flame for 4 to 5 minutes. Place in serving bowls and garnish with strips of toasted nori and minced parsley.

Somen with Lemon and Watercress in Chilled Broth

> 2 packages somen (16 oz), cooked and rinsed
> 4 to 5 lemon wedges, for garnish
> 1 bunch watercress
> 4 to 5 cups water, including kombu and shiitake soaking water
> 1 strip kombu, 2 to 3 inches long, soaked

**4 to 5 shiitake mushrooms, soaked, stems removed, and
   quartered
2 to 3 Tbsp shoyu
water, for boiling watercress
1/4 cup black sesame seeds, toasted, for garnish
1/4 cup scallion, finely sliced, for garnish**

Place the kombu, shiitake, and water in a pot. Cover and bring to a boil. Reduce the flame to medium-low and simmer 5 minutes. Remove the kombu and set aside for future use. Cover and continue to simmer another 10 minutes until the shiitake are tender. Add the shoyu, reduce the flame to low, and simmer 5 more minutes. Remove the pot from the burner and allow to cool slightly before refrigerating. When the broth is chilled, remove from the refrigerator. While the broth is chilling, place 1 inch of water in a saucepan, cover, and bring to a boil. Add the watercress and cook 1 minute. Remove and let cool or very quickly rinse in a strainer to cool. Place the somen in serving bowls and ladle the chilled broth over the somen. Garnish each bowl with a slice of lemon, 1 to 2 teaspoons sesame seeds, several sprigs of watercress, and chopped scallion.

Pasta Vegetable Soup

**2 cups corn elbows or ribbons, cooked and rinsed
4 to 5 cups water, including kombu soaking water
1 strip kombu, 2 to 3 inches long, soaked
1/2 cup onion, diced
1/4 cup green peas, removed from shells
1/4 cup daikon, diced
1/2 cup carrot, diced
1 cup tofu, cubed
1/4 cup celery, diced
2 to 3 Tbsp shoyu
1 bunch watercress, cut in 1 inch lengths**

Place the water and kombu in a pot, cover, and bring to a

boil. Reduce the flame to medium-low and simmer 5 minutes. Remove the kombu and set aside for future use. Add the onion, green peas, daikon, carrot, and celery. Cover and simmer 5 minutes. Add the cooked pasta, tofu, and shoyu. Cover and simmer 4 to 5 minutes longer. Add the watercress and simmer 30 seconds. Ladle into serving bowls.

Quick Ramen in Broth

> 2 packages instant whole grain ramen (from natural
>   food store)
> 2 packets instant broth (included in package)
> 5 cups water
> 1 sheet nori, toasted and cut in thin strips, for garnish
> 1 cup tofu, cubed
> 2 to 3 Tbsp scallion, finely sliced, for garnish

Place the water in a pot, cover, and bring to a boil. Add the ramen and cook, uncovered, for 3 minutes. Add the instant broth and tofu. Simmer 1 to 2 minutes. Place in serving bowls and garnish with strips of nori and sliced scallion.

Pasta Fagioli (Pasta and Beans)

> 2 cup whole grain elbows, shells, or other small pasta,
>   cooked al dente,
> rinsed, and drained
> 1 cup navy or white kidney beans, soaked 6 to 8 hours
> 1/2 cup pinto beans, soaked 6 to 8 hours
> 4 to 5 cups water
> 1/2 tsp sea salt
> 1 Tbsp extra virgin olive oil
> 1/2 cup onion, diced
> 1 to 2 tsp umeboshi vinegar
> 1/4 cup scallion, finely chopped, for garnish

Place the beans (discard soaking water) and fresh water

in a pressure cooker. Cover and bring up to pressure over a high flame. Reduce the flame to medium-low and cook for 45 to 50 minutes. Remove from the flame and allow the pressure to come down. Remove the cover. When the beans are done, heat the oil in a pot and sauté the onion for 3 to 4 minutes. Add the cooked beans and juice. Mix and add the sea salt and umeboshi vinegar. Cover and bring to a boil. Reduce the flame to medium-low and simmer for 10 to 15 minutes. Add the cooked pasta and simmer another 5 minutes or so. Place in serving bowls and garnish with chopped scallion.

6
Fish Soups and Chowders

Fish soups and chowders are hearty and nourishing. They complement your whole grain and vegetable dishes, and are wonderful on special occasions. Try to use fresh fish and seafood when preparing these dishes. Cooking fish in soup makes it softer and more easy to digest than broiling, grilling, or deep-frying. The contracting effects of fish are counterbalanced somewhat by the vegetables and vegetable juices used in the stock. A small side dish of grated raw daikon or horseradish also helps to balance fish dishes. Vegetarian readers can still prepare these recipes by using tempeh, tofu, dried tofu, fu, or seitan instead of fish or seafood.

Trout Carrot Soup

2 freshwater trout, insides removed, but leave head and bones intact
carrot, equal in volume to trout, cut in matchsticks
water, to cover ingredients (2 inches above)
2 tsp light sesame oil, for sauteing carrots
1/2 to 1 tbsp barley miso per cup of water
1 to 2 tbsp fresh grated ginger, for garnish
1/4 to 1/2 cup scallion, finely chopped, for garnish

Cut the trout in large chunks. Heat the oil in a pressure cooker. Sauté the carrot for 2 to 3 minutes. Place the trout on top of the carrot and add enough cold water so that it is about 2 inches above the ingredients. Cover, place over a high flame, and bring up to pressure. Reduce the flame to medium-low and cook for 60 minutes. The bones should become soft. Remove from the flame and let the pressure come down. Remove the lid and place back on the stove over a low flame. Add the puréed miso and simmer, without boiling, for 5 minutes or so. Place in serving bowls and garnish with 1/4 teaspoon ginger and 1 to 2 teaspoons chopped scallion.

Oyster Miso Soup

4 to 5 cups water, including kombu soaking water
1 strip kombu, 2 inches long, soaked
5 to 6 fresh shiitake mushrooms, stems removed and
    quartered
2 cups daikon, cut in thin matchsticks
1/4 cup carrot, cut in thin matchsticks
1/2 to 1 lb fresh shucked oysters
1 pint fresh clam juice
4 to 5 tsp white or yellow miso, puréed
1/2 cup snow peas, cut in half on an angle
1/4 cup scallion, finely chopped, for garnish

Place the water, kombu, and clam juice in a pot. Cover and bring to a boil. Reduce the flame to medium-low and simmer 5 minutes. Remove the kombu and set aside for future use. Add the shiitake, daikon, and carrot. Cover and simmer for 3 to 5 minutes. Add the oysters (either whole or chopped), cover, and simmer 1 to 2 minutes. Reduce the flame to very low and wait for the water to stop boiling. Add the miso and snowpeas, cover, and simmer, without boiling, for 2 to 3 minutes. Place in serving bowls and garnish with chopped fresh scallion.

Summer Fish and Vegetable Soup

4 to 5 cups water, including shiitake soaking water
4 to 5 shiitake mushrooms, soaked, stems removed, and
  diced
1/2 cup onion, diced
1/4 cup celery, diced
1/2 cup fresh green peas, removed from shell
1/2 cup fresh sweet corn, removed from cob
1/4 cup green string beans, cut in 1 inch lengths
1/4 cup yellow wax beans, cut in 1 inch lengths
1/4 cup carrot, diced
1/4 cup daikon, diced
1/4 cup leek, sliced into thin rounds
1 lb white meat fish, cut in chunks
2 to 3 Tbsp shoyu
1/4 cup parsley, scallion, or chives, finely chopped, for
  garnish

Place the water and shiitake in a pot. Cover and bring to
a boil. Reduce the flame to medium-low and simmer 15 minutes. Add the onion, peas, beans, celery, corn, carrot, daikon,
and leek. Cover, turn the flame up to high, and bring to a boil.
Reduce the flame to medium-low and simmer for 5 to 7 minutes. Add the fish, cover, and simmer 3 to 4 minutes. Add
shoyu, cover, and simmer another 5 minutes. Place in serving
bowls and garnish with parsley, scallion, or chives.

New England Clam Chowder

1 lb fresh clams, chopped and minced
1 pint fresh clam juice
4 cups water
1/2 cup onion, diced
1/2 cup celery, diced
1/2 cup carrot, diced
1 cup turnip or rutabaga, diced

1 to 2 Tbsp corn oil
1/3 to 1/2 cup unbleached white flour
1/4 to 1/2 tsp sea salt
1/4 cup parsley or chives, minced, for garnish

Heat the oil in a pot. Sauté the onion for 2 to 3 minutes. Slowly add the flour, stirring constantly until the flour completely coats the onion. Sauté for 1 to 2 minutes. Slowly add the flour and clam juice to the sautéed onion, stirring constantly to prevent the flour from lumping. Stir until the liquid becomes thick and creamy. Next, add the celery, carrot, turnip or rutabaga. Cover and bring to a boil. Reduce the flame to medium-low and simmer 10 minutes until the vegetables are tender. Add the sea salt, cover, and simmer another 5 to 7 minutes. Add the clams, cover, and simmer another 5 minutes. Do not over-cook the clams or they become tough and rubbery. Place in serving bowls and garnish with parsley or chives.

Manhattan Clam Chowder

1 lb fresh clams, chopped and minced
1 pint fresh clam juice
4 cups water
1/2 cup onion, diced
1/4 cup celery, diced
1/2 cup carrot, diced
1/4 cup cabbage, shredded and minced
1 small red pepper
1 Tbsp umeboshi vinegar
1/4 tsp sea salt
2 tsp extra virgin olive oil
1 dried bay leaf
1/4 cup parsley, minced, for garnish

Cut the pepper in half and remove stem and seeds. Place on a cookie sheet and bake at 450 degrees F. until the skin is blackened. Remove from the oven and peel and discard the blackened skin. Dice the pepper very finely. Place in a blender or food processor with a few drops of water. Blend into a paste.

Heat the oil in a pot and sauté the onion for 2 to 3 minutes. Add the water, clam juice, bay leaf, celery, carrot, and cabbage. Add the pepper purée. Cover and bring to a boil. Reduce the flame to medium-low and simmer 10-15 minutes until tender. Add the sea salt and umeboshi vinegar. Cover and simmer 5 minutes. Add the clams, cover, and simmer 5 minutes. Remove the bay leaf and discard. Place the chowder in serving bowls and garnish with chopped parsley.

Clear Broth Soup with Fish Dumplings

4 to 5 cups water, including kombu soaking water
1 strip kombu, 2 inches long, soaked
5 fresh shiitake, stems removed and sliced thin
1 cup daikon, cut in thin matchsticks
1/2 cup carrot, cut in pinwheel or flower shapes
1 bunch scallions, cut in 2 inch lengths
2 to 3 Tbsp shoyu

Fish Dumplings
1/2 lb cod, haddock, scrod, or sole fillets
1/4 cup unbleached white flour
1 tsp sea salt
3 Tbsp mirin (can be omitted)
2 scallions, thinly sliced
4 Tbsp carrot, finely diced
4 Tbsp celery, finely diced
2 tsp black sesame seeds, roasted
2 Tbsp kuzu
2 Tbsp water, for diluting kuzu
1/2 cup whole wheat flour, to roll dumplings in
light sesame oil, for deep-frying dumplings

Slice fish into small pieces and purée to a thick paste in a blender. Remove the paste and place in a mixing bowl. Add the unbleached white flour, sea salt, mirin, sliced scallion, carrot, celery, and black sesame seeds. Dilute the kuzu and add to the mixing bowl. Mix all ingredients until smooth. Place 1/2 cup whole wheat flour in a small bowl. Form the fish paste into small balls about the size of a golf ball. Roll each ball in the flour to evenly coat. Heat 2 to 3 inches of oil in a deep-frying pot. Deep-fry several balls at a time until golden brown. Repeat until all the balls have been deep-fried. Drain on paper towels. Set aside while you prepare the soup.

Place the water, kombu, and shiitake in a pot. Cover and bring to a boil. Reduce the flame to medium-low and simmer for 5 minutes. Remove the kombu. Add the daikon and carrot flowers, cover, and simmer 2 to 3 minutes. Add the shoyu and fish balls. Simmer 3 to 4 minutes. Add the scallion and simmer another 1 to 2 minutes. Serve.

Resources

One Peaceful World is an international information network and friendship society devoted to the realization of one healthy, peaceful world. Activities include educational and spiritual tours, assemblies and forums, international food aid and development, and publishing. Membership is $30/year for individuals and $50 for families and includes a subscription to the One Peaceful World Newsletter and a free book from One Peaceful World Press. For further information, contact:

One Peaceful World
Box 10, Becket, MA 01223
(413) 623–2322
Fax (413) 623–8827

The Kushi Institute offers ongoing classes and seminars including cooking classes and workshops presented by Wendy Esko. For information, contact:

Kushi Institute
Box 7, Becket MA 01223
(413) 623–5741
Fax (413) 623–8827

Recommended Reading

Books by Wendy Esko

1. *Aveline Kushi's Wonderful World of Salads* (Japan Publications, 1989).
2. *The Changing Seasons Cookbook* (with Aveline Kushi, Avery Publishing Group, 1985).
3. *Diet for Natural Beauty* (with Aveline Kushi, Japan Publications, 1991).
4. *The Good Morning Macrobiotic Breakfast Book* (with Aveline Kushi, Avery Publishing Group, 1991).
5. *Introducing Macrobiotic Cooking* (Japan Publications, 1978).
6. *The Macrobiotic Cancer Prevention Cookbook* (with Aveline Kushi, Avery Publishing Group, 1988).
7. *Macrobiotic Cooking for Everyone* (with Edward Esko, Japan Publications, 1980).
8. *Macrobiotic Family Favorites* (with Aveline Kushi, Japan Publications, 1987).
9. *Macrobiotic Pregnancy and Care of the Newborn* (with Michio and Aveline Kushi and Edward Esko, Japan Publications, 1984).
10. *The New Pasta Cuisine* (with Aveline Kushi, Japan Publications, 1992).
11. *The Quick and Natural Macrobiotic Cookbook* (with Aveline Kushi, Contemporary Books, 1989).
12. *Raising Healthy Kids* (with Michio and Aveline Kushi and Edward Esko, Avery Publishing Group, 1994).
13. *Rice Is Nice* (One Peaceful World Press, 1995).

About the Author

Wendy Esko teaches macrobiotic ocoking at the Kushi Institute and around the world. She is the author of *Introducing Macrobiotic Cooking*, co-author with Aveline Kushi of *The Changing Seasons Macrobiotic Cookbook*, and author of *Rice Is Nice* and many other books. She lives with her husband, Edward, a macrobiotic author and teacher, and eight children in Becket, Massachusetts.

Recipe Index

Grated Daikon Soup, 62

Hato Mugi Soup, 35
Hearty Winter Miso Soup, 18

Jinenjo Soup, 69

Kasha Vegetable Soup, 39
Kenchin (Kuzu Vegetable Soup), 67
Kidney Bean Vegetable Soup, 49

Leek and Mushroom Soup, 63
Lentil Millet Soup with Smoked Tofu, 45
Lentil Vegetable Soup, 44
Lima Bean and Fu Soup, 51

Manhattan Clam Chowder, 88
Millet and Corn Soup, 35
Millet and Squash Soup with Miso, 24
Millet and Squash Soup, 34
Minestrone, 48
Miso Soup with Broccoli and Fu, 24
Miso Soup with Carrot, Onion, and Wakame, 12
Miso Soup with Daikon and Lotus Root Dumplings, 16
Miso Soup with Daikon and Sweet Rice Dumplings, 14
Miso Soup with Daikon, Celery, and Tofu, 15
Miso Soup with Daikon, Shiitake, and Greens, 13
Miso Soup with Mochi, 21
Miso Soup with Natto and Grated Daikon, 26
Miso Soup with Sweet Corn, 18
Miso Soup with Winter Squash and Dulse, 22

Navy Bean and Corn Soup, 47
New England Clam Chowder, 87

Oat Soup with Dulse, 40
Oyster Miso Soup, 86
Ozoni (Japanese New Year Miso Soup), 22

Pasta Fagioli (Pasta and Beans), 83
Pasta Vegetable Soup, 82
Pinto Bean Soup, 50
Puréed Broccoli Soup with Tofu Sour Cream, 60
Puréed Carrot Soup, 60
Puréed Cauliflower Soup, 58
Puréed Squash Soup with Miso, 23
Puréed Squash Soup, 59